WITHDRAWN

Advance Praise for *Love Strong*

"Denna is that tough-love girlfriend everyone needs, but not everyone is lucky enough to have. With heart and humor she will tell you straight what role your early childhood messaging about relationships is playing in current your love misfortune—and then how to actually get past it once and for all. She is a Godsend."

—Nicola Kraus, Bestselling
Co-author of *The Nanny Diaries*

LOVE
Strong

CHANGE YOUR NARRATIVE, CHANGE YOUR LIFE, AND TAKE YOUR POWER BACK!

DENNA BABUL, R.N.

SAVIO
REPVBLIC

A SAVIO REPUBLIC BOOK
An Imprint of Post Hill Press
ISBN: 978-1-64293-449-6
ISBN (eBook): 978-1-64293-450-2

Cover Design by Cody Corcoran

posthillpress.com
New York • Nashville
Published in the United States of America

To my daughter Sophie Bleu, may you always know
the power and magic you have within you to love.

To all of the women out there that have struggled in love. I
got you. We got this. It is time to take back your power.

C O N T E N T S

PART III: FOUNDATION FOR THE FUTURE

PART I:
UNPACKING THE PAST

CHAPTER 1

WHO ARE YOU?
WHY ARE YOU HERE?

I once heard that if a woman's father was an alcoholic, she could be in a room with a hundred men and the only one who would catch her eye would be the one with a drinking problem. Why is that? Is it a familiarity that we seek, or something deeper programmed into our DNA? The fact is that our family of origin, the experiences of members of that family, and reactions to those experiences introduce us into a room before we ever even say hello. We are walking stories of our pasts looking to find commonality in others.

At some point in our lives, we are shown a fork in the road. One direction leads us down a road of magic and intense emotion, leading us to challenge our histories, and the other course takes us down a safer path—one that will guarantee perhaps a more guarded life but will also keep our hearts out of harm's way.

You are here for one of two reasons. You took the magic carpet ride, fell in love, and lost your way, leaving you flailing through life looking for another adventure, or you took the safe route and are bored to tears. I have taken both paths, which is why I am writing this book. I want to help you get the love you want by showing you exactly who has been in the driver's seat in your relationships.

It is your subconscious relationship mind that has been making most of your decisions. She is the part of your mind who is not fully aware of what you want but continues to influence your actions, feelings, and many of your choices. You can blame her for your snap judgments, like going home with your ex-boyfriend even though you know you will regret it in the morning, or that "Old Town Road" song getting stuck in your head on a loop all day long. According to most cognitive neuroscientists, we are conscious of only about 5 percent of our cognitive activity, so most of our decisions and emotions depend on the other 95 percent of the brain's activity that is not fully awake.

I AM HERE TO WAKE UP YOUR CONSCIOUS RELATIONSHIP MIND.

We are going to go back through your life and take a look at how and why you made the decisions you made. In doing so, we will attempt to wake up your conscious relationship mind so that she can finally get in the driver's seat. Think of her as your highest emotional self. We want to make friends with her and tap into what she knows in order to take your power back once and for all.

LET'S DISCUSS BREAKING UP

You are here because you want answers. You may have already mastered many aspects of your life and found happiness in those areas. Your career is on point. Your friendships are rewarding, and your mini goldendoodle gives you all the affection and kisses your heart desires, but romantic love is still out of your reach. You are here because you have yet to master the one thing you want most in your life: true love.

Many women today spend the majority of their lives in the driver's seat. Because they may have had to take control early in their lives, it gave them the confidence not only to know what they want but to have the tenacity to go after it; however, in love, wanting it and going after it does not always lead to the best results.

Although you may desperately want to, you can't always make the people you love, love you back. You also can't ask or expect your partner to heal you. He does not know all of your pain and is most likely not trained to help you figure it out. He may want to, and may even try for a time, but eventually he will give up—because while he can enrich your life and grow with you, he can't fix you.

The issue, whether you know it or not, is you, and up until now, you may not have been willing to examine your family-of-origin relationships—or known that you should. So, you may not be fully aware of how much they are ruling your adult relationships. In relationships, the load has to be equal. To have a successful, loving partnership, both people have to a) want it, b) want to work on it, and c) value it. If the equation is off or heavily emotionally weighted on one person, the relationship will collapse under the pressure. Sound familiar?

I am sure you can think back to relationships in your past or maybe think of ones in your present in which the weight was or is solely on your shoulders. The reason for this is that your partner picker is off. Take a beat to reflect on your choices. Have you always chosen people who were ready to give and receive love? Have you perhaps chosen someone who was not willing to give enough, so you turned yourself inside out to try to make it work, only to be left heartbroken for longer than you care to admit? Maybe you have been the one who was unable to give? You thought you were giving, but you were taking. Did you expect too much? Did you want him to heal the inner child in you who still needed protection? These are the types of questions you will answer throughout the book. To get out of your head, you have to heal those parts that are damaged. Healing equals freedom, and freedom equals opportunity. If you don't have the freedom to make real, conscious choices, the opportunities you are desperately seeking will not appear. Instead, you will have a limiting belief of what you deserve. Therefore, you will bring only those types of relationship opportunities into your field of sight. I know it is trippy to think about all of this, but it could not be more accurate.

INNER CONFLICT

Think about what inner relationship conflict has been on a constant loop in your head for years. Where did it originate? What about that conflict is true? How has it been controlling your choices? What healing needs to take place? In short, what theme do you want to kick to the curb that has been seriously underserving you for years? To get you started on your way to freedom and new opportunities, let's look at some common personal relationship conflict themes that might currently be in charge of your subconscious decision-making. These are listed merely for recognition. Do not put a check mark by any of them, because, girl, you are not taking them with you.

- I fear abandonment.
- I fear commitment.
- I am a control freak.
- I am codependent.

- I am afraid to love.
- I love too intensely.
- I am inclined to mother my partner.
- I am overly sexual or asexual.
- I am unworthy of love.
- I have an unreasonable list of expectations for my future mate.
- I am distrustful.
- I feel stronger alone.
- I am afraid to be alone.
- I am scared to be vulnerable.
- I am destined to be alone.
- I can quickly point out issues in other people's relationships but am unable to see the flaws in my own relationships.
- I am too picky.

All of these are horseshit, by the way. They probably origi-nated in your formative years through the unwanted osmosis of your parents' inner relationship beliefs. At some point in life, we have to recognize where to drop off our inner children, though. They can't come to the big leagues. They are just not equipped to carry us to our intended destinations.

MY STORY

My first real romantic relationship started when I was seven-teen years old and lasted until I was twenty-one. He asked me to marry him, and I complied out of fear of losing him. I had already lost the first love of my life, my father, and walking away from my second love seemed unbearable. My inner conflict was fear of abandonment. I allowed my subconscious to take the lead in all aspects of my life. I was just too broken, and staying on the surface was safe.

We were married on July 18, and by August 6, I fled, feeling suffocated by my life's already being planned out for me. I remember being in the hotel room of our honeymoon suite in the middle of Disney World feeling like my life was coming to an end versus just getting started. I was profoundly depressed and snuck off to call my mother from the lobby. "Mom, I want to come home. I don't think I should have gotten married."

My mom took a deep breath and lamented, "I thought this might happen." I remembered our talk in her kitchen about a month prior when she had told me I did not have to get married. We were putting together the programs for the ceremony. Each one had to be folded together at the crease and flattened to lie correctly. As I stacked each one neatly on top of the pile, I could feel a deep sadness coming over me. "I miss my dad," I said, knowing the mere mention of his name had the ability to change all of the energy in the room. I continued, "It just does not feel right. I mean, to get married without having a father to walk me down the aisle." I could feel all of the emotion flying up my throat, ready to erupt.

"Are you sure this is about your dad, honey?" my mom asked. "You know you don't have to get married, right?"

I wanted to scream. It *was* about my dad. I needed him. I needed his love. A father is supposed to protect his daughter from making bad decisions. I wanted him to stop me, but he couldn't.

I felt like I was watching someone else's life and not my own that day in Florida when I told him I was leaving. I broke him. The guilt would stay with me for years. I did not know who I was, nor did I have any idea how a normal, healthy marriage was supposed to look. I walked into forever with not a single relationship tool or coping skill. Seeking safety over love, I got married because I thought that was what I was supposed to do, not because I wanted to. I simply wasn't strong enough to look for magic.

My parents had not done me any favors in the relationship department. They had a tumultuous marriage, which ended in a bitter divorce. In the thirteen years that I had my father in my life, he seemed broken. Alcoholism had taken over all of his hopes and dreams, and on his best days, I got a sober man who was hoping to get his life back on track. He struggled to find his place, and before I could get to know him, he passed away, leaving me to try to fill in the blanks.

My mother would never remarry.

My mom inherited her issues from two parents who chose alcohol over their children, forcing her to be a fiercely independent woman who took pride in not needing a man. According to her, her "picker was off," and she seemed to pick only men who lacked drive or ambition. She was and still is a ball-buster. She attracted men who seemingly needed to be tamed. When she broke them, she would lose interest. The one she could not tame was "the guy." I watched her go from not wanting him to chasing him for years.

If we can look a gift horse in the mouth, we heal. If we don't, we continue down a path of uncertainty, with our subconscious leading the way, wondering why we have not gotten the love we want. The cycle, just like my mother and father's, can be passed down for generations. It takes one brave soul to break it. I was that brave soul in my family tree to take on that challenge. I implore you to do the same. You are here because you are raising your white flag. You are brave and ready to get this love thing right. If you are willing to do the work, the universe will pay you back with love like you have never imagined.

MY STORY CONTINUES

After leaving my first husband, I ran right into the arms of another man. He was a college football player full of ego, testosterone, and other hormones. He lived about forty-five minutes from where I had grown up, and for me, that was like the other side of the world. I wanted to run away from my issues, and his arms offered me a soft place to land.

Spending time with him far away from everyone I had ever known gave me the new start I so desperately wanted. It allowed me the refuge to believe that I was okay. But after nine months of mind-blowing sex, his jealousy and my fear of commitment started to overshadow our physical connection. I could no longer act like I had my shit together. I could no longer run from myself and my issues. Just like Julia Roberts in *The Runaway Bride*, I had been taking off in search of anything or anyone who could save me because I was not ready to protect myself. I was exhausted, confused, and looking to fill the void left so long ago by my father. I wanted to be loved, yet I had no idea how to give or receive the love I so desperately wanted.

Bored with the ongoing relationship issues, I wanted to find something I could excel in. I decided to focus on my future and anything I could to avoid the mirror. I enrolled in nursing school, swearing off men for the foreseeable future. It wasn't my lifelong dream to become a nurse, but I'd taken a personality test to see what I might be suited for, and the results had come back that I would do best in a field that helped others. So, off I went. Again, I was taking the safe route and ignoring the magic.

Nursing school was a bit harder than I expected. I had to move home to make ends meet, and that took me back to all of the memories and unanswered questions I'd had since childhood. Although my mother and I were close, she was alone, financially strapped, and still focusing on "the guy" who had gotten away. She was refusing to look in the mirror. Instead, her new mantra was that she did not need a man. She was fine alone. I made a mental note that started the process I would one day use to heal myself: Don't get trapped chasing a man who does not want to be caught. Have the guts to do the work. I wanted a different life for myself. I was determined to make it happen. The drive was there, but the emotional work had not yet begun.

After I left the football player, one of his buddies called about a month later to ask me out. I had barely noticed him before. He seemed nice, almost too nice, and I reluctantly agreed to go on a date with him, mainly out of boredom. I was my mother's daughter and ready for a little subconscious fun. After our first lackluster date, I tried letting him down quickly and recommitting to my schoolwork. I said, "Look, I had a great time. I am just not ready."

But he persisted. And I was too mentally exhausted to put up a fight. He was kind enough, and boundaries were not yet my forte, so I acquiesced, back in the safe zone. He drove the hour and a half from his house to my mother's a few nights a week, brought food, rubbed my aching feet after I had been standing in the hospital all day, and made plans for us on the weekends. He gave me pep talks when I did not believe in myself. He did everything humanly possible to make me fall in love with him… only I don't think I ever really did.

Three years later, I married him, for reasons even I did not completely understand. That marriage also ended in my leaving him. It took two failed marriages, a hell of a lot of emotional anguish, and a move to an entirely different state alone for me to find the courage to go in search of myself. I was starting to see my reflection in the mirror.

I took my nursing degree and the small amount of dignity I had left and set out to change my life once and for all. The process was not without its setbacks, heartbreaks, or challenges, but I did the work. Healing is a process, just as falling in love is a process. Many women want the easy fix. We grab a stack of self-help books, go to a few therapy sessions, and take advice from our friends, believing we are evolving into what we need to be to find love.

Instead, we have to go back and unlearn the parts that don't help us and replace them with new techniques and coping skills that do.

I almost titled this book *Why This Guy* because the person who finally stumps most women is that one guy or girl who makes you turn yourself inside out to land him or her. The one who leaves you so you can find yourself. I know this was the case in my life, and I have seen it be the case in the hundreds and hundreds of women I coach. My story will continue to unfold in this book, as will the stories of other women. I challenge you to find parts of yourself in these women. You may be heartbroken right now, but I encourage you to see this as a gift. Take the time to commit to loving and learning about yourself. I dare you to believe that you can find what you are looking for—both in yourself and in a significant other.

LOVING STRONG

After way too many sleepless nights, surveying my tribe on social media and asking every single person I know, I decided to change the title to *Love Strong*. The definition of "strong" is something along the lines of having the power to move heavy weights, perform physically demanding tasks, and being able to withstand great force and pressure. My guess is that along the way, you have tried your absolute best to keep up with the demands of a challenging partner or relationship by contorting yourself in every way possible to make the relationship work. You have most likely had to withstand an abundant amount of pressure from family and friends when going against their advice and staying in a relationship that did not suit you. Think about the strength it took to love someone else so unconditionally that you may have lost yourself along the way. How about if you pivoted that amount of love and strength back to yourself right now? What would it look like to find a strong love built from the coming together of two stable and powerful hearts?

You know when you go to the wedding of a couple who have such an undeniable love that you know they will make it? When you see them together, you see they are complete magic, and even apart, they have just as much power. That, my sister, is the essence of strong love, the unbreakable confidence of a woman who knows her worth and will stop at nothing until she finds a mate who knows his, too. The knowing is the gift. In that knowing, you don't have to push and prod to get the love you want. It exists easily without wavering or strife; it is the purest form of love. You deserve that. To me, strong love is the only love. Everything else is just a speed bump along the way.

We have all felt weak in a relationship at some point in our lives, in romantic love or maybe even in friendship love. The weight of the relationship's not working out can cause a person to falter. He or she may start to wonder, "Am I the problem—or is it the other person who has the problem?"

Many times, as women, we take on the brunt of the blame. We are born to nurture, so we get busy taking care of another person's needs, and somewhere along the way forget about ourselves. We may think, "If I could just love this person more, it would all work out." We set about trying to understand how to love the person better and start forgetting about self-love. When the balance is off or somehow shifted to favor the other person, that is weak love. It is not sustainable, and in order to keep it going, we will inevitably lose ourselves in the process. Think about a past relationship, the one you are in now, or the one you are hoping to gain in the future. How do you want to feel? How do you not want to feel? To give you a better understanding of the difference between loving weak and loving strong, I have listed a few characteristics below. Think about your person. Circle which category your love falls into based on how it made or makes you feel.

Loving strong can:

Empower you.
Restore you.
Bring peace and love into your life.
Give you the confidence to both give and receive love freely.
Treat you kindly.
Accept you in all of your glory.
Make you happy.
Encourage you to try new things.
Make you feel secure.
Give you hope.

Loving weak can:

Make you question yourself.
Make you feel sad.
Make you feel misunderstood.
Make you act out in anger.
Make you feel fear.
Make you close yourself off from family and friends.
Make you change who you are.

Make you question who you are.
Make you feel crazy and out of control.
Make you feel unlovable or unworthy.

By putting these defining characteristics on blast, you can start to see where you are beginning your journey with me. Have you settled? If so, don't beat yourself up, sister. The past is the past. Period. You don't live there anymore. We are not here to feel shame about who we are or where we may have come from. We are here to accept change. My job is to help you understand why you keep picking the same types of partners, how your family ties into those choices, and how to shift your narrative to take your power back and learn to love strong. As Brené Brown, PhD, says, "Owning our story can be hard but not nearly as difficult as spending our lives running from it. Embracing our vulnerabilities is risky but not nearly as dangerous as giving up on love and belonging and joy—the experiences that make us the most vulnerable. Only when we are brave enough to explore the darkness will we discover the infinite power in our light."

To help you stay on track and in the light, I have put together ten defining statements. Write these down and repeat them every time you start to let that pretty little head of yours wander off.

- I am the curator of my own love life.
- I focus on my goals and don't get distracted by misalignment.
- I don't have time for negative self-talk.
- There is nothing stronger than a woman willing to rebuild herself.
- Self-care always comes first.
- My personal truth is that I deserve to love strong and be loved strongly.

- I have all that I need within me to be loved and give love.
- I am responsible only for myself.
- I can let go of what or who no longer serves me.
- I am not broken.

It is time to focus on yourself, babe. You are made of love, power, and grace. Make a promise to yourself to go this journey with me without judging yourself or your past choices. Shower yourself with mercy and allow the power to rise within you as you learn more and more about what got you here and how to start anew.

CHAPTER 2
WELCOME TO THE PROCESS

You are here because you are in conflict; the conflict is either within yourself or with someone else. You don't know if you should go back to him (or stay with him) or even if he wants you to. Your head is exploding, and you want off the roller coaster.

You may be on an island all alone. You may have initially started on a sabbatical of finding yourself by cutting off your dating life, only to put yourself back out there to realize not much has changed. Either your picker is off or the types of men you are drawn to come around only once in a lifetime...or so you think. It is time to take the bull by the horns. You are in charge of your destiny. You can't let someone else create your life's vision plan. It is just not a good look.

LET'S GET STARTED

At a certain point, the problems many women acquired in childhood begin to stare back at them, demanding to be dealt with. My coaching clients fight this, and I sympathize—the last thing any of us wants to do is work on ourselves to fix something our mother or father may have impressed upon us. They, too, did not ask to be a product of dysfunction, heartbreak, or confusion.

But when humility comes knocking—when some breakup, or ghosting, or rejection is the last straw—these women become ready to see that some part of their childhood came with fallout. And typically, that is the daddy part—or, more so, how the momma-and-daddy part did not work. Whatever your own particular circumstances, it is your family of origin and their experiences that shape how you, in turn, learned to relate to other people in your interpersonal relationships.

The women who work with me run the gamut. Some have fathers who are absent, while others have fathers who are present. Some women were reared by single mothers, and others have helicopter moms. Some have parents who, whether one or more of them is an alcoholic, a workaholic, or a rageaholic, are in the family home physically, but may not be present with my clients in a way that created a good template for relationships. This can be a confusing juxtaposition for women. You can love your mother and your father but still have some issues with them at the same time.

This is not to imply that you are screwed because of your parents' possible issues. This book is merely asking you to take a really hard look at how your family of origin's relationships play a big part in how you handle relationships as an adult.

WHERE DOES THIS LEAVE YOU?

The woman who comes to me for coaching may think that her current situation is why she is here, but most likely her ongoing conflict started many years ago.

She may be missing her dad. Perhaps she feels if it weren't for his death setting her back, she would be doing okay right now. Maybe she is a daughter who still holds a lot of resentment toward her mother because of things the mother did or did not do while she was growing up. Perhaps she has a pretty good relationship with her dad but in no way wants the same relationship her parents have with each other. Possibly she thinks her mother was not the best at picking partners or was a doormat. Whatever the case, she wants to keep the past in the past and live in the present. She wants to do things differently. Well, guess what? We all do. But to be different, she has to be willing to take a deep dive into her past. The woman I am speaking to wants to do some spring cleaning because she has a life to lead, and love is the center of that equation. So, buckle up. We are about to get down to business.

Frequently women fall into the trap of putting all of their energy into working on their imperfect partner instead of working on themselves. It's called projection. It's when we take our problems or pain and put them onto someone else, precluding us from having to deal with our issues. Projection can give us a false sense of security. "It's not me who's the screw-up; it's the person I've chosen to love. But because I am the ultimate giver, I have decided to fix her or him and not myself." It can be a way of protecting ourselves when we are not ready to face our issues, or perhaps it's something we're completely unaware of. Sometimes it takes experiencing the same heartbreaks over and over again to finally decide that enough is enough.

The way to know if you are projecting is simple. Ask your friends to call you out when you do it. For example, I have a client, Hannah, whose father is very much alive and very much detached. To people on the outside, it would look like a healthy father-daughter relationship, but it's all surface. When she calls, he asks about the weather before handing off the phone to his wife. She has taken that subsequent abandonment into her adulthood and become extremely self-sufficient, unaware that her father's years of brushing her off are playing a massive part in her adult relationships. She makes her own money, and although she does not flaunt it, she is telling the universe, "I don't need a thing from a man; I can take care of myself."

She has been married twice to two versions of her father. Each husband was financially driven—so much so that they could never give her what she needed most: time. Time is her love currency.

Unfortunately, she had not done the work to understand that when I met her. Instead, she spent years trying to teach each husband just how messed up he was. She even sent them both to see her favorite marriage counselor in the hope of "fixing" them. When her second marriage ended in divorce, she was at her wit's end and confided her grievances to me. I came back with a simple statement: "Have you ever thought it might be you who needs counseling?"

Not only had Hannah chosen projection as a form of not having to look within, but she also took on the persona of the accommodating type. She grew up learning to survive by neglecting her individual needs. Instead of focusing on herself, she became self-sacrificial to keep all things in her life copacetic.

Accommodators routinely yield to another's point of view, even when deep down they may have a different opinion. They are often attracted to big personalities who can carry the load of entertaining, planning, and handling the big things, like finances or running a company. For Hannah, both of her husbands could do those things, much like her father, yet when it came to giving of themselves and creating a true partnership, the intimacy was just not there.

EXERCISE: DETERMINE YOUR CONFLICT STYLE

We all have a go-to conflict style, usually born out of the subconscious teachings of our parents. You may have gotten your love for battling from your father or your need to compromise from your mother. Whether you are a lover or a fighter, it is time to look at how you deal with conflict. As you are going through this exercise, think back to your last relationship. Pick out your style but also notice your parents' method. Do they match up? Think of how your parents did or did not deal with conflict. Was there usually a resolution? Do you see any patterns in your life as compared to your parents' lives? As you read through these, you will start to see how your romantic partners might be perceiving you. Have you been understood? Have your intention and direction met up? What is your final destination? Hint: It is where you are today.

The purpose of this exercise is to find yourself in these descriptions, but you will also start to identify others along the way. I love my Determine Your Conflict Style exercise. I seriously could write about it all day long. My friends and clients have gotten so used to my using it that they can even diagnose themselves. It is a beautiful day when someone from my tribe starts the conversation like this, "So you know I am an Avoider…"

Put a check mark beside your style.

> **The Battler:** When in conflict, you pursue your concerns at the other person's expense, using whatever means you need to win. You compete by standing up for what you believe in (even if it is a bit "holier than thou"), defending your position, or merely trying to win.
>
> When is this cool? It works when you need to make a quick decision. Like when your part-

ner can't decide if he or she wants Mexican food or Italian, and you make the call instead of driving around for an hour "hangry." It also works for circumstances like enforcing important rules for your children or when unpopular decisions are being made at work.

When is this not cool? When you want your partner's real opinion without fear or judgment.

Kate is a Battler. Her style is something that works for her in her corporate world. She likes being aggressive, and it has helped her climb the ranks in her law firm for years, even helping her make partner in record time; however, it has proven to be an issue in some of her relationships. Here is Kate's story in her own words:

I have always had an opinion about everything. My college boyfriend was a momma's-boy type. We met while I was in law school. He was a rugby player who stood six-foot-two with a stocky build. On the field, he was a take-no-prisoners type of player, but off the field, his demeanor was that of a giant teddy bear. Because I like to challenge other people's opinions, I thought I had met my match.

We went strong for about six months, until we had a huge blowout fight at a party. We were playing pool against another couple, and he made a terrible shot. It made us lose the game, and I called him a punk in front of everyone. A few people laughed. Eddie walked out of the room and slammed the door. When I found him in the backyard, he was not happy with me.

"Why would you embarrass me in front of everyone like that?" he griped.

I could not believe how over-the-top he was being. I said, "Really? You can't take a little friendly competition?"

With that, he threw my keys out into the yard and said, "You are relentless!"

It took me two hours to find my keys. I was livid and let him have it for the rest of the night. I called him every name in the book, and when that did not get a rise out of him, I went after his mother. I know I shouldn't have, but she was the reason he could not man up. She taught him some of that old childish BS, like if you don't have anything nice to say, say nothing at all. He had no coping skills. When we had a disagreement, he went mute. Most of our relationship was like that. I would get annoyed, tell him how much he annoyed me, and he would sit there and take it or shut down completely.

When we broke up, he said something that stuck with me and has resonated in every one of my relationships ever since. "Kate, you play dirty. You fight to win, whereas I fight to make things better. With you, no one can ever win, so why should they even try?"

Eddie was right on many levels. Battlers only fight to win. Therefore, the other person always loses. Not exactly a recipe for a healthy, long-lasting relationship. Kate has had to learn that her conflict style, which she picked up from her mother, has allowed her to both continue to be right and continue to be single. It may have worked in securing her partnership in her law firm, but in her relationships, it has crippled her.

> **The Helper:** You can be both assertive and collaborative. You genuinely want to find a resolution that both parties can feel good about. You feel safe to dig deeper into an issue to uncover concerns you both have to find alternatives to meet each other's needs. By collaborating, you gather essential insights to stop any competing views or unwanted, heated confrontations.
>
> When is it cool? When you want to find resolution and have to work through hard issues that could interfere with the health of your relationship.
>
> When is it not cool? Know your audience. Make sure you don't put the other person into sleep mode by discussing things ad nauseam. As a side note, I am a Helper, and my husband may or may not have a tinge of narcolepsy (not really), so I have to make sure I choose my time wisely for conflict resolution, like not in bed, because he will begin to snore past the four-minute mark.
>
> **The Balancer:** You like to compromise. Compromising is the middle child between battling and accommodating (see below). You give up a little more than the Battler but are not quite accommodating. You look to find an answer that both parties can live with even if you have to give a little. The Balancer spends some time exploring a partner's concerns and splits the difference.

When is it cool? For minor issues when you want to achieve a temporary decision.

When is it not cool? If you are undermining your partner and trying to fix a more significant issue without really doing the work, which happens a lot in today's world. Put your phone down or have a specific time each day to check in with each other hands-free—unless it is a sexy time, of course.

The Avoider: You are not usually assertive and can be uncooperative. Because you don't address conflict, you withdraw or side-step.

When is it cool? When an issue is not important—although classic Avoiders usually tell me breakup stories like "He would not let my dog sleep in the bed, so I left him." Translation: "We had been avoiding the real issues for so long that when my golden retriever was ignored, I'd had enough." This is cool only when you don't see a real reason to fight over something you don't have all the facts on.

When is it not cool? You don't ever have an opinion, so he quits asking. Ask yourself, are all decisions placed on his shoulders? No one wants a bump on a log. Make sure your views are heard. What you have to say matters.

Soon after I first started doing relationship coaching, I met Suzanne, a single mother with a taste for the wrong men. Every guy she had a relationship with was either married or morally or financially bankrupt. Suzanne came to one of my seminars but kept her arms crossed the entire day. You could tell she was pissed.

The more I talked about how past issues get in the way of current relationships, the more uncomfortable I could tell she became.

At the end of the seminar, she waited at the back until every last book was signed and the room had cleared out before approaching me. This is nothing new. Although many women speak up at live events, telling their life stories or the conundrums in their current relationships, there are still some who feel more comfortable one-on-one. Suzanne was an introvert, more of an observer than a person who commanded attention. In her relationships, I would label her the Avoider type. Avoiders are usually unassertive and can be uncooperative, too. When Avoiders are in conflict, they typically fail to pursue their concerns and those of their partners. Therefore, they are always on the losing end of any argument.

After we made small talk, I asked her what was on her mind and how I could help. She explained her situation something like this: "I live with someone, and our relationship is just not working out. I'm not happy, but I'm also scared he's going to leave."

I asked her: If she wasn't happy, would his leaving be such a bad thing?

But she wasn't ready to hear it yet. Classic Avoider mentality. She had unknowingly been handing over her power, and it was only a matter of time before their relationship would hit the skids.

Of course, a few months later, he left her.

She arrived at my office, devastated. She said, "I was single for five years before Matt. I guess I'm destined to be alone."

I asked her if that sounded like anything in her family-of-origin dynamic. It turned out her mother had divorced her alcoholic father in the mother's early thirties and had never been in another relationship, growing lonelier and more embittered and regretful with every passing year. The subconscious takeaway for

Suzanne: Men are hard to find. You have to hang on for dear life. Avoid conflict at all times.

I worked with Suzanne for the next six months to take a real look at her relationship history. She had to ask herself, "Why am I here?"

Over time she worked through the process and finally went on to have a healthy dating life, and even reconciled with her father along the way. Just a few months ago, I asked Suzanne to tell her story at one of my seminars. I could not believe the butterfly she had become after crawling out of that stagnant cocoon she had wrapped herself in so tightly. Even my cameraman noticed. I have had the same cameraman for audiovisual work for several years. He rarely gets invested in the stories of the women who attend because he is so busy running around changing microphone packs. But when Suzanne spoke, he listened.

He came up to me on the break and commented on the change he had noticed in her. He said, "She seems like a different person. She sat up straight and was very engaged, unlike the last time. She seems happy." I listened intently but had other things on my mind. I wondered, would they make a cute couple? I can't help myself sometimes.

> **The Accommodator:** You don't assert yourself, and you cooperate at all times. You don't get your needs met because you don't pursue them. You are seen as overly generous and obey even when you prefer not to.
>
> When is it cool? When preserving harmony is essential. Example: When you don't want to go to the same chain restaurant that his mother likes every Sunday, but you do it anyway.

When is it not cool? When you feel that your feelings don't merit the attention they deserve. Deferring too much can deprive you of your voice for things that are important to you. Speak up.

EXERCISE: MAKE YOUR ROAD MAP

Purchase a journal or notebook, one that speaks to you with colors that evoke power. Then pick a time and place in your home to focus on just you. Feel free to decorate the place you pick with flowers, candles, pillows, or anything that makes you feel happy and comfortable. Be intentional.

Now that you understand your conflict style, it is time for your first homework assignment.

1. Write down your relationship history.
2. Write down the name of each person you have been in love with so far. Leave a blank page after each person's name for future homework assignments.
3. What first attracted you to each person?
4. Write down your conflict style and the conflict styles of your previous partners.
5. What made your relationships work, and what did not? List the reason you broke up with each person from your point of view.
6. Write down the reason you broke up from his or her perspective.
7. In one sentence, write down what you learned from each relationship conflict style.
8. List ways you could have communicated differently.

I know. It is an eye-opener. You may already be able to see that a relationship went on longer than it should have or how it was destined to fail because of lack of communication. Warning: This work may make you want to reach out to a few peeps in your past to show them your newfound knowledge. Don't do it. We are just getting started. There are many more epiphanies to come.

PUT TOGETHER A RELATIONSHIP COUNCIL

Now I would like you to put together what I call your relationship council. A relationship council is composed of two to four people whom you trust to have your best interests in mind. You are going to ask them to give you their feedback on your relationship history. Don't reveal what you wrote; ask them to answer the same questions as you did and send the answers over to you. Revealing is part of healing. Acknowledge that this feedback is helping you to become more conscious. Trust your council.

You are beginning to build the blocks of self-awareness and break down why you keep doing what you are doing in relationships. By doing the above homework, you will start to gain some much-needed perspective on what has happened in your relationships. You may even begin to notice a theme. What is your calling card? Where are you on the dating curve? What are you putting out there? How is it working for you? Acknowledgment is the first step in recognizing where you may be getting stuck.

These assignments will give you guidelines on what you need to look at to understand your role in the dating/relationship pendulum. Patterns dominate, and you can become trapped by them unless you get perspective. It's essential to target and break down the behaviors that are getting in your way. By understanding the common themes in your relationships, you will start to make small changes, and that is progress.

CHAPTER 3

WHERE RELATIONSHIPS ARE BORN: YOUR FAMILY OF ORIGIN

I always knew my single mother had reached her highest level of stress when the words "I can't take this anymore. I am going to have a nervous breakdown" would come shooting out of her mouth after a hard day. When I was a child, those words signaled my brother and me to stay out of her way. We instinctively knew that whatever was causing her the stress would eventually shut her down if we did not give her some space. What usually followed was her going to her room with a migraine, or in some cases a girlfriend of hers would come over to help her talk through her grievances. Today, as two grown adults, my brother and I will sometimes laugh when she starts in with her "I can't take it" claims. To us, her coping skills need some refining, but to my mother, her emotions are genuine. She is a verbal communicator and needs to discuss things ad nauseam to figure them out. Ask any man I have dated, and he will tell you I got the need to overanalyze from my mother. I will tackle any subject from a host of different angles until I figure out the answer. Thankfully, it has paid off for me in my line of work.

Many people think a relationship is born when they meet the man or woman of their dreams. The truth is that how we behave in relationships and what we expect in relationships—of ourselves and of our partners—start long before our eyes ever meet in a crowded room or we see his or her profile online. Just like my mother and myself, you too have a style of communicating that you learned from your family of origin.

The messages your family gives you about relationships are powerful and can affect everything about how you go about giving and receiving love. The things we hear and see can leave an imprint on our mind and, most important, on our heart. Depending on your family, you may have picked up verbal cues that play a significant role in your life today. Put a check mark by any of these that bring up any emotion.

Verbal cues:

"Never be alone."
"You don't need a man."
"Have somebody, or you are nobody."
"Be independent."
"Stay in a relationship, no matter what."
"Financial security is everything."
"Make him chase you."
"I can't handle stress."
"Change is bad."

Your parents may not have actually said any of these phrases out loud, but the way your parents interact (or not) and speak to each other (or not), and how they value, treat, and relate to each other set you on a path for how you will appreciate, manage, and interact in your relationships. And, in turn, how you will expect to be valued and treated. Nonverbal cues are just as important as what we hear. If your parents never fought, how can you know how to handle adversity or conflict?

Think about the nonverbals in your household when it came to love. Were the birthday or Christmas presents your parents gave each other practical or exciting? Did your parents go on dates? Did they show passion by kissing, holding hands, or snuggling? Were they good communicators? Did they talk about their feelings openly so that you could see that conflict can lead to resolution? Could you see how they made up? One of my clients says she knew exactly when her parents were having sex at night because the radio in their room would come on full blast for about fifteen minutes before she heard the shower start up. It may have grossed her out at the time, but by hearing that radio crank up, she knew they were still in love and all would be okay.

Take a minute to write down the verbal and nonverbal cues you received while growing up. Here are a few more to get your memories flowing.

Nonverbal cues:

You never saw your parents kiss.
Your parents never argued.
Your mother rolled her eyes anytime your father told a joke.
Your mother never dated.
Your father always drank beer on weekends.
Your mother always carried the groceries inside alone.
Your father never "took up for himself."
Your family members were not big huggers.
Your mother did whatever your stepfather wanted.

Although I knew I was deeply loved in my family, we were not big huggers. For us, showing affection was done by telling stories and spending time together laughing and joking. What I figured out as an adult is that my "love language" is spending time together, while my husband's is verbal affirmation along with physical touch. Because my mother was very verbal, I was continuously told where I stood, that I was worthy and also that I was beautiful. Yes, I was lucky in that way; however, what I was not taught was that physical touch is a big part of showing affection. Hugging is something that did not always come entirely naturally to me. I had a boyfriend or two tell me along the way that I was more like the guy in the relationship when it came to needing affection. It did not click with me until later, when a friend of mine on my relationship council pointed it out to me. She said, "Why don't you ever hug me when I see you?" I laughed it off until I realized she was right. I had been a bit stingy with my affection, and although I felt the love for her, I did not necessarily know how to show it other than verbally. For months after her callout, we would hug it out when we first saw each other and when we were saying our goodbyes. It may sound corny, but that little shift opened my eyes to what I and others may also need in relationships.

Knowing if you are a verbal or nonverbal communicator can save you from a lot of heartbreak and confusion. All of these verbal and nonverbal cues in life were the building blocks of your foundation in relationships. There are pros and cons to both. Nonverbal communicators can sometimes come across as aloof, whereas verbal communicators can talk too much. Think back to a past relationships and how you communicated with each other. Did you take the time, or did the relationship go south because of a lack of understanding? Once you've identified how you and a partner learned to communicate, things will flow much better.

As I write this, I am struck by how the cues my husband and I both learned in childhood are still playing out in our current lives. With our kids, I am more of a communicator, asking them how they feel about any given subject. I connect through words, whereas my husband shows how he feels by the quality time he spends with our kids, even though there may not be much talking going on. Because I know our histories, I can take it for what it is worth and see the positives in both styles. On a side note, the very first song I listened to on repeat was "You Talk Too Much" by Run DMC. Coincidence? I think not.

TRIGGERS

Decoding past relationships (including the one with your dad) can help you figure out the *who* and *why* of your dating style and relationships. Triggers are a big part of that decoding. Triggers cause emotional knee-jerk reactions based on past unhealed or learned experiences that may have absolutely nothing to do with the present situation and everything to do with transporting you back to your original trauma. They can impede the natural flow of a relationship and cause you to react in a way that seems ill-matched to the situation at hand. By identifying those triggers, you can start to connect the dots as to why you respond in a certain way, and begin to find healthier solutions.

One young lady I met and later coached had a constant need to be validated. She and her then boyfriend were connected at the hip. She even sat right up beside him in the front seat of his truck when they drove places. They were in round-the-clock contact every day. Even when we would meet for our sessions, she would talk to him right up until the moment we started and then call him the moment we finished. I listened as she told him about the most mundane things, like the flowers she had just seen or what she had eaten for a snack. She came to me to figure out how to keep her relationship going in a good direction and not to have it end like all the other ones. Upon getting her family relationship history, I realized that both of her parents had never been alone. They both had divorced and remarried multiple times in record succession. Like her parents, she went from relationship to relationship. When she grew tired of one, like magic, a new and seemingly improved guy would appear. She would break it off with one person and jump into a relationship with the next one almost unfazed. One of her nonverbal cues from childhood was never to be alone. Although she was not directly told that, watching her parents act it out had made a big impression on her, affecting how she went out into the dating world.

In the present day, when a boyfriend starts to slip from the intensity of the new love into the more mundane day-to-day style, she is triggered into thinking the relationship is over—because of her parents—and just picks up and starts up with someone new to stay in that intense new-love phase where she feels safe.

Understanding my triggers was a monumental step forward for me in my process. Even though I saw myself as being as cool as a cucumber in relationships, I soon realized that I was not nearly as put-together as I thought. Because I did not react out of jealousy like some of my other friends, I assumed I did not have trust issues—but I did. I quickly learned that my triggers were centered around follow-through. I did not trust that a man would always do what he said he was going to do. My mother had chosen men, starting with my father, who would inevitably let her down.

My father was a dreamer, a big proponent of making elaborate plans that would never come to fruition. One Christmas he promised both my brother and me orange mopeds. Don't judge; I was into orange at the time. Anyway, I proceeded to tell all of my friends in the neighborhood about this orange moped that would be delivered to yours truly on Christmas Day. By noon on Christmas, something in me had changed. The moped had not arrived, and even I could no longer carry on the charade that my dad was just too busy on a work trip. The truth was, he had not followed through on his promise. My trust was broken.

What I learned was that men can and will let you down. For many years I chose men who could not hurt me. They loved me more than I loved them, so I stayed in the safe zone in my early relationship life, as you have read.

It wasn't until I met "the guy" that I learned I had a whole lot of work to do on myself. I chose someone who was not ready for a commitment. I should have known it from the start. I mean, we met on a cruise. He was with an entire fleet of single men, and I was with two married friends and one who was about to get engaged. I was newly single and ready to mingle. He was just ready to mingle, and would just mingle for many years to come. We traveled together and played together for the first year, partying almost every weekend and having fun. I knew I was in over my head when I felt things should become more serious, and he started pulling away. The more he pulled away, the harder I worked to keep him. I just wanted to be chosen. Finally, my dignity stepped up, and I broke things off with him right before I was about to pick up my life and move to a different state to be with him.

Alone back in South Carolina, I tried to get back out there and date, but the pool of men was not doing it for me there.

I wanted adventure, but being with my ex was all I could think of. One Friday night a few weeks into our breakup, I got a call on my cell phone. "Can I come see you tonight?" he asked, a little buzzed. My heart leaped out of my chest. "We are already on I-20 about an hour away," he continued.

I tried playing it cool and said, "Sure. You can stop by for an hour or so." I jumped up from my bed and hurried around, picking up all of the pieces of depression debris scattered around my apartment.

We got back together that night. My defenses dropped to their knees the minute I opened the door and saw those big brown eyes staring back at me. Things went well for the next few months, and just after Christmas I packed up my belongings, rented a U-Haul, and moved to Atlanta. A month after I arrived, we started arguing again. I wanted to play house while he just wanted to play. Soon he was back to his old ways. I was becoming triggered each time we made plans and he canceled to go out with his friends or on a trip with the guys. Again, I was not chosen. His follow-through was that of a sixth grader, not of a man who was serious about me and our future. After too many breakups to count, we ultimately fizzled out, but not before he crushed me. There I was in my late twenties and more mixed up than I had ever imagined was possible. I had put everything into this one person and not into myself. But our destructive relationship was the mirror I needed to finally force myself to look at myself. In it, I saw a broken little girl who had never dealt with the real man who had first broken her heart: her father.

After a few years of gut-wrenching therapy, I connected the dots and understood why I had gotten to the place I was at in my life. By the time I met the man who would later become my husband, I was working on my first book, *The Fatherless Daughter Project: Understanding Our Losses and Reclaiming Our Lives*, and had just started a nonprofit. I felt I was doing my life's work and was ready for a real adult-style relationship. I thought my issues had been dealt with and were tucked away in a cute little corner.

But a few months into the relationship, my inner control freak came out to play. I was still my parents' daughter, and the years of programming by them were still lying just under the surface. I wanted to be chosen, and when I got triggered, my need to ensure that would happen would take center stage.

For example, when my husband and I were dating, he would always be late to pick me up, and I would lose it, derailing the entire evening. To me, his being late meant that I was not important enough for him to show up on time. I had not altogether connected the events of my life at the time, so he must have seen me as controlling when in reality I merely needed time to believe that he was going to do what he said he was going to do.

I used my verbal communication skills to dip my toe into the uncertain relationship waters. I told him about my father and how his lack of follow-through made me feel vulnerable and insecure. He said, "I understand and will try to communicate better when I am going to be late." We have been together for over two decades now. I want to say he is never late, but I would be lying. In time, I had to realize that it was just who he is. He wants to accomplish a lot on any given day, and sometimes his time-management skills do not work to his advantage. The takeaway here is that it was up to *me* to keep doing the work and not bring my old triggers into our relationship. The work never stops. We are constantly evolving and ever-changing human beings. Our past comes back to us in the form of triggers, and it is up to us to decide to let them go. You may not be in control of someone else's actions, but your reactions to that person's actions are solely up to you, my friend. My husband has chosen to stay. He is my rock. My friends even gave him the nickname "Concrete" because no matter what, he is always there. He calls me "the Warden." Go figure.

I hope that you, too, will find your concrete. Now almost twenty years into my relationship with my husband, many of these issues seem like a distant memory. We have had to learn to communicate effectively and honestly to keep the romance alive.

I tell you all of this to remind you that no matter where you are in your life right now—single, married, or on a sabbatical from romance—you can and will find true love. All you have to do is get yourself all polished up in the trigger department before you swipe right.

Some triggers are not very deep and can easily be avoided. In today's culture, social media is a big trigger for so many people. We are practically forced to publicly announce to the world that we want to break up with someone or no longer be friends with someone. While social media has been the birthplace of so much good in the world—like bringing attention to worthy causes, raising money, and connecting people—it has also caused some harm. What I know for sure is that social media is not the place to air your dirty laundry. Don't share your innermost pain in a meme or passive-aggressive quote. If you do that, you are allowing people close to the situation and people who aren't in your daily life to judge you up close and from afar.

Trust me, you don't need the peanut gallery when you have a relationship council and a family who can give you the love you need and want. My advice to you is to take a social media break anytime you feel vulnerable or susceptible to unfavorable reactions. You are too cool to do otherwise. Don't let anyone or anything control your mood and set you off. This book and this time in life are all about you taking your power back!

SIGNS

While triggers can be connected to past trauma, signs are not.

We all have gut instincts, a sixth sense or, as some people like to call them, signs that are trying to get our attention in relationships. You know, that flicker of conscious thinking that keeps trying to tell us to watch out—yeah, we are talking about that one.

The fight-or-flight response was first described by an American physiologist named Walter Cannon, who realized that a chain reaction occurs in the body to deal with a dangerous circumstance. In response to acute stress or real perceived danger, the body will signal a warning by triggering a whole host of hormones to be activated. In turn, heart rate, breathing rate, and blood pressure will increase to facilitate what we need to fight. This response can happen if we come upon a bear in the woods or see a fire erupt. Believe it or not, the response can be triggered even by imaginary threats. The stress of any perceived danger is there to help us cope better under pressure. The body gears us up to either survive the threat or flee the situation for safety. I like to think of signs as the universe's way of trying to elicit a fight-or-flight response to a not-so-good situation.

I am sure you can conjure up a time when the threat of danger warranted a real fight-or-flight response. I also want you to think about times in your relationship history where your body reacted to a perceived risk, like catching someone cheating on you or having to say goodbye to someone prematurely. Were there signs leading you toward the inevitable ending?

Many women and men I have coached had signs when it came to turning points in relationships—ones they chose to ignore or that made them flee. In the movie *Ghost*, Whoopi Goldberg's character, Oda Mae Brown, has been posing as a psychic for years when she finally sees a ghost: Sam, played by Patrick Swayze. Scared to death, she tries to ignore Sam, but he won't let her. He is trying to communicate with his wife, Molly, to warn her of impending danger. Oda Mae is so stunned, she blurts out, "Molly, you are in danger, girl!"

The cool thing about the universe, our conscious mind, and our gut feeling is that they, too, are a part of our council looking to warn us when our subconscious is being a little brat and trying to take center stage. Here are a few of the classic signs people have shared with me when it came to the universe or their gut trying to steer them away from a bad situation. Take stock in these stories. If you see yourself in any of these, you may be in danger, girl!

Jude, 36

I was dating this guy for a couple of months during one of the most insecure phases in my life. He was very experienced, while I was still naive to the whole gay-nightclub scene. I had just moved from rural Louisiana to the city and was too intimidated to hit the clubs. I sensed he was not faithful, so one night I decided to spy on him from my neighbor's car. I drove right up to the railroad crossing where the club was just on the other side of the tracks. I sat there for a while willing myself to cross those tracks, park my car, and go in and find him. I saw a few men walking arm in arm across the street and could make out one was Stewart. My palms started sweating, and I started breathing faster. I stepped on the gas, flooded the car, and it stalled out right on the tracks. Just then, the red lights started blinking. I had to think fast so I would not get hit by an oncoming train. I jumped out on adrenaline and pushed the car out of the way. When I knew I was safe, I leaned my back against the car door and slid down and slumped to the ground. My gut told me to leave him alone, or I would get hurt. I let him go that night. I also never drove a stick shift again.

Lorean, 28

I bought a black BMW convertible after Marc and I broke up. I changed everything in my house to remove the memories of us. I bought a new bed, changed the comforter set, and painted my room lavender because I wanted to feel calmness around me. Every trace of him was gone with the exception of the hole he left in my heart. We were off and on for almost three years. He seemed to be getting along just fine except for the random late-night drunk calls where he would say stuff like "Do you miss me?" while pulsating music from the nightclubs blared in my ears. I deserved better than him, and I knew that. I could not get him out of my head. We had talked about marriage and kids. Our families had met. All of our friends were intertwined, and starting over just seemed useless.

I decided that the only way to get over him was to fall off the face of the earth. I shut down all of my social media, blocked his number, and started hanging out with girls from my office. Things were starting to look up. I wasn't crying as much anymore and had even turned off the Hallmark channel and started watching Netflix when I got the call. "I'm engaged, sister!" yelled Becca on the line. "And guess who is going to be a bridesmaid?" I started praying to the heavens that it was not me.

"Me?" I said, trying to muster up some cheer. Becca was marrying Stewart's best friend, Gunner. We would both be in the wedding party.

The day of the wedding, I was feeling in control. I thought I was ready to face Stewart and strong enough to be cordial if nothing else. I decided not to bring a date, and the plan was for me to leave early. No wine, no crime. We made it through the wedding and to the reception without me speaking to him. He looked so handsome, though. I was sitting at the bridesmaid table staring off into space when I felt someone come up behind me. I could smell his Tom Ford cologne before I even turned around. He placed a single dark chocolate truffle down in front of me—my favorite. I thanked him. Made small talk and got away to find Becca. I was crumbling fast. He said so many beautiful things to me. He missed me. He was sorry it had not worked out and wished we had never broken up. By the end of the night, I had given in to temptation and was slow-dancing with him on the black-and-white checkered dance floor. As the crowd faded, I found myself hand in hand with him walking out to the valet stand. In the distance, I could see my little black convertible staring back at me, summoning me to get in her and drive away.

"Come home with me," he said while dipping me back to kiss me. My head said no, but my heart was saying yes. I went home with him.

We had a fantastic night, probably because of the six glasses of wine that were giving me liquid courage.

The next morning before I even opened my eyes, I regretted it—all of my progress gone in one night. We ended up having the same argument over breakfast we'd had for the last year. I wanted to get married. He wasn't ready. As he drove me back to the reception venue, I felt the shame devour me. Why had I allowed myself to fall back into his trap? I was hurt, and he was unscathed.

As we pulled into the private driveway, I could see the tail end of my car. "Nice car," he said, trying to lighten the mood.

"Thanks," I murmured, almost in tears. When I turned my head to see my car, I noticed a huge dent where someone had sideswiped the driver's side. There she sat in all of her beautiful glory fractured and alone, just like I was. I felt a knowing come over me. A sign was telling me that this would be my future with him. I would continue to get hurt while he would continue to walk away. That was the last night we ever spent together.

Selena, 40

I dated, got engaged, and almost married Robert, a cop, inside six months. For me, he symbolized what was right in the world. He saved me from the years of being a single mother and doing it all on my own. But a few months in,

I started seeing some cracks in his armor. He was misogynistic, and my daughter seemed to be going within herself around him.

The turning point was when a friend of mine was over meeting him for the first time and witnessed him yell at my daughter for spilling Coke. She later pulled me to the side and said it was all she could do not to punch him. She cautioned me about marrying him and told me to talk to my daughter about how she felt.

I broke it off with him but regretted it almost immediately. I did not want to be alone, yet I questioned the man he was. We started talking again some, and things were moving into the direction of us getting back together, until one night I saw his old partner from the force sitting at the bar. Against my better judgment, I decided to stop and say hello. After a few beers, Barry told me what had happened. He had caught Robert sleeping with his girlfriend the night after we got engaged. When he confronted him, Robert cut him off completely. I was so thankful I saw Barry that night. His words were the final nail in Robert's coffin. I swear the world works in mysterious ways.

I ran into Robert's sister-in-law about five years ago. I told her all about my husband and the beautiful daughter we now had. She said, "It's a good thing you did not marry Robert. I know how much you wanted another child, and we came to find out he's sterile!"

Be aware of what you are putting out into the universe. If you have a problem, the universe will aid you in finding the resolution you need to heal. Look out for those signs. Not all signs are bad, and not all triggers are real; however, it is vital to understand your history to know what may emotionally trigger you. Being aware of these things can help you to communicate your needs better and begin to guide you to understand what trauma you may still need to deal with.

EXERCISE: IDENTIFY YOUR TRIGGERS

Below are some possible triggers. Put a check mark beside any trigger you recognize. In your journal, write down any others that come to mind for each partner you have had.

Potential triggers:

He or she will not fully commit to you or give you what you want.

He or she is flirting with someone else and being disrespectful.

He or she is lying to you or is possibly not being entirely honest about a situation.

He or she is not answering the phone or texting back in a timely matter.

He or she is using drugs or alcohol and loses control.

He or she is verbally, emotionally, or physically abusive.

He or she makes commitments and doesn't follow through on them.

Now I want you to write down any triggers each of your parents has. It may help to think about what behaviors they seem to react to the most. Here is an example:

I have a client named Shawn, who is well into her forties and struggling with trust in her marriage. Her backstory is that her parents' marriage ended after an affair her mother had with her father's brother. It is a fact that Shawn likes to keep hidden.

All through her twenties, Shawn dated a guy who was a serial cheater. She tried everything in her power to control the situation—from giving ultimatums to spying on him at random times outside of his apartment. A few years after that relationship ended, she met and married her current husband.

The first year was like a honeymoon. Shawn felt that all of the drama from her past was over. She saw herself as normal now that she had managed to land the right guy. But slowly her insecurities started to creep into the marriage. It began with her keeping close tabs on him when he went to play pickup basketball on Wednesdays. She would send him flirty text messages and wait for him to respond to quiet her anxious mind. It then escalated to an expectation that he stay in constant contact with her during the entire day, even when he was at work. The newness was wearing off quickly, and her husband was beginning to pull away, saying he felt suffocated.

When I met Shawn, she brought her husband along. He was eager to understand why his wife had changed seemingly overnight. Over the years, I have worked with countless men who have lovingly wanted to know more about why their wives' father issues seemed to be randomly showing up in their current relationships.

I explained to Mike that her issues had always been there; she had just been working incredibly hard to keep them at bay. I told him plain and simple, "She still ultimately fears abandonment. Her distrust of marriage runs deep. Because her mother cheated and her father just stood by, she wants to make sure you will a) fight for her and b) never cheat on her." I reiterated that it was not his cross to bear but that it was vital for him to tread lightly around the issue.

We worked on understanding her triggers as part of the process. Today, Shawn is aware of the work she needs to do to deal with issues from her childhood, and luckily for her, Mike is a keeper. He calls me periodically to ask for advice on how to deal with specific situations, and I feel good about their marriage because they both want to understand each other. In a partnership, if both parties want the same thing, anything is possible.

Now fill in the blanks in these sentences:

I get triggered when

_____.

I react by

_____.

The reason I do this is

_____.

A healthier way to react would be

_____.

My defining statement is

_____.

Shawn filled in the blanks like this:

> I get triggered when my husband ignores me and is unresponsive.
>
> I react by spiraling and demanding answers and constant contact.

The reason I do this is that I am fearful he will eventually leave me.

I want him to validate his love and respect for me by staying in constant contact.

A healthier way to react would be to trust him and remember my defining statement that we worked on with Denna: He will be in touch when he is able. He loves me, and that will never change.

A defining statement is a truce, if you will. It is a narrative shift that you can say out loud or practice in your head when your anxiety shoots up from one of your old triggers. If you are in a relationship, it is a statement that you both can agree on that is true to the situation. By doing this, you are consciously deciding to change your narrative and shift your thoughts to a more positive outcome. In turn, you will be taking your power back by redefining your past triggers and not allowing them to play out in the present. It takes a little bit of practice, but the emotional payoff is worth the work.

If you are single or just in an early phase of dating, like I was, it may look something like this:

I get triggered when the guy I am newly dating ignores me and is unresponsive.

I react by spiraling and demanding answers and constant contact.

The reason I do this is that I am fearful he will eventually leave me.

I want him to validate his love and respect for me by staying in constant contact.

A healthier way to react would be to trust my defining statement: I trust *myself* and need to remember that new relationships take time to evolve. We are in the learning process. I am equipped with my core traits and will know if and when I should go or stay.

We will get into core traits in a later chapter.

Be honest, but don't throw up all of your issues on him. When he calls, ask him if he has gotten your messages and wait for him to fill in the blanks. If you have a seed of doubt, pull in the people on your relationship council. Have them vet it. These moments are typical at the beginning of a new romance. They can be quickly resolved with both parties feeling better and more understood.

If you are in a current relationship and getting triggered, play out the triggering scenario in your head. Figure out why you're getting triggered by using the Identify Your Triggers exercise above. Are you being triggered by a specific pattern? If so, can you use one of the conflict styles to work through it? If the answer is yes, then sit down with your partner and figure out a defining statement to help bring you back down to earth. In Shawn and Mike's case, Shawn's defining statement was: "He will be in touch when he is able. He loves me, and that will never change."

Now, if you are triggered because of something your partner is doing that is detrimental to your relationship, that is another story. Involve your council on this one. Ask yourself if your partner has your best interests at heart. If you question that, even for a minute, it may be time to make some difficult decisions.

Here's the thing: Sometimes it's about who we are dating or married to, and sometimes it's about us. There can be patterns to our dating lives and relationships that we don't see (although our friends can see them very clearly, as I am sure you learned with the previous homework assignment).

It's tough to see the pattern when you are caught up in the middle of it, so some perspective on the patterns and types that you have dated or are dating will help you see where you are and how to break any habits that aren't working for you.

Experiencing triggers is like weighing yourself on a scale. They are there to remind us when we may be overdoing it or not doing enough to take care of our hearts. Sometimes it takes dismantling some of our learned beliefs and reactions to those beliefs to see what it is that we want in a mate.

By taking the time to look at who we are and have been in our past relationships, we begin to find the clarity needed to decide what works and what doesn't. Don't trip. This is all part of the process. Decoding your trigger patterns will make room for new and improved relationship skills and reactions. Remember, you are here because you deserve a bigger love. Although these exercises may bring up some things you would rather keep buried, they are a crucial part of the process.

CHAPTER 4

WHO'S YOUR DADDY?
WHO'S YOUR MOMMA?
WHO'S YOUR GANG?

Have you ever turned on your favorite entertainment news channel and heard yet another story about a famous woman who seemingly is being "done wrong" by yet another man and wondered what was going on in her head? I have, and many times I've been able to trace it right back to a malfunction in her relationship locator. Famous or not, we have all picked the wrong man at one time or another. As they say, stars are just like us. We, too, have relationship issues that other people in our lives may be scratching their head about, wondering why we keep falling into the same traps with the same types of men.

WHO IS YOUR GANG?

I am sure that stars like Khloé Kardashian have gotten an earful from their inner circle about what they should and should not do in relationships. The problem is: women tend to surround themselves with other women who have the same relationship issues or values. We need our lady pack, but at times it can be like the blind leading the blind. Many times, women give advice from their current vantage point. Take, for example, any of the *Real Housewives* series on Bravo. Inevitably, one lady ends up telling another lady she drinks too much or has an alcohol problem while simultaneously taking a shot of liquor herself to try to "deal with a situation." Does that make sense to you? It may be entertaining, but is it helpful? My point here is that you are in a growth period. You are trying to shed your battered relationship skin for a shiny new coat. Don't listen to people who are entrenched in the same types of battles. Surround yourself with real mentors who have found love and come out on the other side. They are where it is at. For now, think of me as your fairy dating godmother/mentor. I want to give you some insight into why you (and perhaps your girlfriends) may keep getting tripped up on the same types of guys or on that one particular guy you or they can't seem to shake. Taking your power back comes from making educated choices to get the outcomes you ultimately want in love and life.

You are still in the discovery process of figuring out why things have not worked out in the love department. Your relationship council is paramount in helping you ascertain and acknowledge the reasons you may be in the spot you are in. Take some time to think about who you are surrounding yourself with, not just in love but also in friendships. It may be time to shake things up a bit and shed not only a few men in your life but also some friendly advice.

EXERCISE: TEACH, PREACH, OR BREACH!

Have you ever played the game Marry, Love, or Kill? Andy Cohen sometimes plays it on his show *Watch What Happens*, and my friends and I have played it for shits and giggles many times in the past. Here is the premise: A person names three people. Then you have to choose one to marry, one to love, and one to kill. Although unseating your relationship council is not as black and white as the game, it is necessary when taking advice from a few of your sisters on Skid Row. I am in no way telling you to drop any of your gang; however, I am advising you to take a good hard look at who you are taking advice from.

For this purpose, let's change the game to picking the people in your life you want to take advice from. Take a second to write down whom you are currently taking advice from, solicited or unsolicited. If a person is capable of imparting wisdom to you in a way that is educational, put the word "teach" beside his or her name. Put "preach" next to the names of the people in your life who advocate for you to take action for the greater good. Put "breach" next to the names of those whom you may have lost confidence in due to their failure to observe issues in their own lives and/or show no willingness to take action to make them better.

For some of you, the idea of knowing whom to listen to moving forward will elicit a strong response that will lead to a shift in the way you do things. Others of you may need to respectfully ask some willing advice givers to let you take the lead moving forward, assuring those people that you are taking a new path. Ask those friends to please respect your new venture. This situation often comes up with my coaching clients and their friends, parents, and other family members. Together we come up with a go-to sentence or two to shield against any unwanted advice or opinions.

An example of a go-to response we usually use goes something like this: "Thank you for your love and support while I am trying to figure out this part of my life. The best way you can continue to support me is by trusting that I can and will make the right decisions for myself through this process. I am taking the means necessary to work through all of this with my coach. I still want you in my life but would ask that you respectfully keep your opinions to a minimum while I do this for myself." The exciting part of this step in the process is that when you take the lead, some of your friends will follow suit. They will see you taking your power back and want to jump on the bandwagon with you.

Below is a list of the types of friends who can drastically help during this process. If you have a gap on your council, now is the time to add to your pit crew.

The relationship council to the stars (you being the *superstar* here):

> **The Purposeful Friend:** She is the one who lives her life on purpose. She is focused on her goals and empowers you to work intentionally toward yours. You would be embarrassed to tell her that you slipped up and went home with your ex. Yes, keep her around. She can be your accountability partner. Let her in on what you are trying to accomplish here. Ask her to be a part of it.

> **The "I Want What She Has" Friend:** This may be a mentor, a work friend, or even a friend you met at church. She has a healthy, loving relationship in her life whose foundation was built on trust and respect. Ask her how she got there. Find out about her boundary process.

What are her deal-breakers, and why? Ask her how she knew her girl or guy was the one.

The Warden: This is the friend who knows you the best. She understands why you do things even before you do, because she has lived your life with you. You go to her when you want brutal honesty.

The Listener: This friend is the best. She follows you around the park or gym while you work out or sits while you eat and listens. She does not judge. She is just there ready to empathize or pay close attention to you while you analyze any situation. She is an invaluable part of your relationship council and should get an award.

The Opposite-Sex Friend: Every girl needs the opinion of a man who does not have an ulterior motive. Yes, men and women can be friends! And we all need a guy in our troop who can call out the duds. I have always had a few of these in my posse. When I was going through my life-altering breakup with "the guy," my guy friends made me pay them a dollar every time I brought up his name. Talk about humiliating, but it worked. With their help, I recognized just how embarrassingly obsessed I was with my guy.

The Impromptu Friend: You know the one who will take off on a moment's notice? This is her. She is always down for a road trip and does not sweat the small stuff. You need this kind of friend to remind you that there is an entire world out there just waiting to be explored.

The Mentor: This friend or guru can guide you through your process. She has seen it a million times, lived it, and become an expert in the space. She will help you navigate the pitfalls and celebrate the wins. She is an intricate part of the process and can show you that you can change your life. In case you are wondering, you can have more than one mentor. Mentors are life-changers.

How does your gang measure up? If you are like most women, you already have a very tight-knit group of friends to take refuge in. Thank God for our girlfriends! They keep us sane and entertained. With the above listing of what I think the members of a good relationship council are, you can take a quick inventory of whom you are listening to. You may already be in the best hands possible, or perchance you need to refocus to align your council with your intentions moving forward. The people we surround ourselves with play a vital role in who we are. Our parents, their opinions, and their DNA imprint also contribute in a substantial way to both who we are and whom we fall in love with.

YOUR FAMILY OF ORIGIN

Dear old Mom and Dad. When it comes to picking a romantic partner, our parents' relationship is at the core of many of our cyclical traps. In this chapter, we are going to focus on Dad first and then Mom.

Fathers come in all shapes and sizes and with all temperaments, but there are a few dad types that are relatively common. Having a dad whose behavior follows that of some of these types can have a significant impact on how you date and relate. One of these descriptions may sound just like your dad, or he may resemble a few of these types. Whatever behaviors and patterns he displayed during your childhood influenced how your relationship locator was set up for adulthood. Before you can reset the locator, you need to figure out what behaviors led you to take a particular direction. Knowing where you came from (and whom you came from) can help you figure out where you should be going.

Take Tanisha, for example. At our first session, Tanisha presented as stuck, exhausted, and hopeless in the love department. She had set all of her hopes and dreams on a man who could not commit because he was already committed to someone else. Cedric was married and going through the most prolonged divorce in history. He was dragging it out by throwing up roadblocks to signing the papers and being done with his marriage. He had one foot in and one foot out. Poor Tanisha and her enormous heart were hanging on his every word, just waiting for the day that Cedric and she could become a real couple and get on with their lives.

Growing tired of waiting for him to cut the cord and spending yet another holiday alone, Tanisha finally decided to bring in some reinforcement in the form of my help. The first thing she needed to consider was one of my core principles: A confused man cannot and will not bring you clarity. You can say "amen" here; I just did. The second thing she needed to understand was the origin of this confusion about whose needs to put first, his or hers. It was abundantly clear to me, but not to Tanisha, that all of her man issues started with her father.

Her parents had never married. Her mother got pregnant in her late thirties by a man who was in his midfifties. Her father was a playboy who had never intended to settle down. He showed up when it was convenient for him, showering Tanisha with gifts once or twice a year. He was generous with his wallet but stingy with his time. Tanisha had learned to take what she could get from men. Her subconscious belief was: "I am too needy. I have to keep my wants and desires at bay to be loved." Well, I called bullshit on that whole scenario, and we got down to business. We worked together for six solid months on the exercises in this book, helping Tanisha understand her worth and how to get the love she both wanted and deserved. But it was when I asked her to write down her and Cedric's relationship story that a bell finally went off.

Her mother was still deeply in love with her father, who had also kept her on a string for years by coming in and out of her life between relationships. He paid for her house, her car, and other necessities, but he had never chosen her. Tanisha had failed to see the similarities because Cedric had proposed. Cedric, unlike her father, was offering a commitment, even though there was no actual date set. She had the ring, but she did not have the man. Once Tanisha connected the two stories, she could see herself in a whole new light. She understood that her father was the Abandoner type, which made her the Settler type.

Tanisha became determined to break the cycle her mother and father had created. She set some boundaries and told Cedric what she wanted—with conviction in her words. Tanisha was ready to change her life. In those six months, she had become an entirely different person.

Soon Cedric was history. With all of her newfound knowledge, she was able to see clearly what she did and did not want in a relationship. I stayed in touch with Tanisha, as I tend to do with all of my clients. About a year after the breakup with Cedric, she attended her high school reunion, where she and her first love picked right up. Today, they have four kids and are nauseatingly happy. By identifying her dad type, she was able to connect her past and present to gain clarity on how she wanted to navigate her future relationships free of her parents' imprint.

Statistics have shown that the same-sex parent plays a vital role in our lives. A common belief is that fathers have a strong influence on their sons' behavior, while mothers have a stronger impact on their daughters' behavior. Gender identification is a crucial part of building a child's personality. It begins almost immediately and follows us into adulthood. Any positive or negative comments made about a child's same-sex parent will have lasting consequences for the entire family.

But it is seen as critical by researchers and therapists alike to allow a child to develop a positive and robust relationship with the other parent. If you are a child of divorce, separation, alienation, addiction, or abuse, I encourage you to take the time needed to heal your inner child's wounds. If not, they will follow you into your adult relationships until you take the valuable time required to repair them. It is not always a walk in the park, but you don't want your fifteen-year-old inner-child-self trying to navigate your thirty-five-year-old's relationship obstacles. She is just not fully equipped to do so.

YOUR DAD'S TYPE

Each dad type has a certain influence and impact. How your relationship played out with your father when you were young (even if he was not in your life) still sways you today. If your dad died when you were young, or your parents divorced or he was otherwise absent from your life, that void where Dad would have been standing creates a relationship type.

It can be a tricky landscape full of what I like to call fun mirrors. If you have ever been to a state fair or a *Ripley's Believe It or Not!* traveling show, you may have had a chance to play in front of one of those mirrors. If you stand in front of a fun mirror, it distorts your image, rendering it long and tall or short and wide. It is the same with men. They may look different and have different jobs, but they still have the power to provoke you.

Here is Katy's story. Katy met Joel, a drummer, at a concert and they became inseparable from that first night, despite the many red flags. Joel was an addict. He drank to cure stage fright and took uppers to stay up all night. At first it was fun, as Katy had spent her life playing it safe—so much so that her previous boyfriend had nicknamed her "Sister Catherine" because of her strict rules around partying and letting loose.

I met Katy at a women's retreat where I was one of the speakers. After I shared my own story about being a Fixer, aka codependent, Katy had a lightbulb moment. For the next few weeks, we spoke multiple times a week about her life and relationship history. Katy was already a rock star when it came to boundaries and morals, but she floundered when it came to hurting someone else's feelings. She was ready to break up with Joel yet scared of what might happen to him without her around.

We worked on a plan, and slowly Katy saw how little control she had over Joel. When she finally connected her need to save Joel with her guilt over not being able to save her father, her life changed dramatically. We dusted off her boundaries, set her intentions, and passed the torch back to Joel to protect himself. He went to rehab and worked on himself, promising Katy to come back to her a better man. Joel is now eighteen months sober and my biggest cheerleader. He has sent me countless clients as a favor for helping both him and Katy make it through the storm. I love a good love story!

Below you will find a list of father types with the corresponding effects they typically have on a daughter. Take out your trusty highlighter and identify your father type and your reaction to it. Keep in mind, you may see yourself in more than one. The fun does not end here. In the following chapter, we will continue to build on this by identifying the types of men you are choosing and why.

Who Is Your Daddy?

The Fun Dad: He may just be a weekend dad since the divorce, or perhaps you won the lottery and he is part of your nuclear family. With the Fun Dad, everything is about overabundance and living without boundaries. The unfortunate part is that your mother probably got stuck with the role of disciplinarian. When there is a lack of balance in the two parenting styles, the children end up picking a style early on, unbeknownst to them.

(You) Ms. Unbalanced: You took on one of your parents' styles and may try to parent your partner like your mother parented your father. If you went the other route, be sure you are not failing to thrive and settling because you want someone to take care of you.

The Overly Cautious Dad: He is scared to death that you are going to get hurt. He probably stood on the sidelines in gymnastics biting his fist every time you took a tumble. He is an overprotector.

(You) the Dependent: You don't take chances in love because you were never allowed to fail. You want to be independent but feel you need a partner. You may fall in love in the early stages of dating for security before getting to know the real person.

The Authoritarian: He told you what to do and when to do it. He thought by keeping you in line he was doing his job as a father, but his lack of emotional involvement in your life causes great pain.

(You) the Pleaser: You seek male attention at any cost. Any attention is good attention. You do what you think a guy wants because you have no idea how to connect on an emotional level with men, and you feel you still can't relate to your father. You probably don't make many demands on others as to how they should treat you or act. Letting others take the lead is all you know, but what do you know about yourself? At some point, you will probably find yourself in a controlling relationship, unable to get your emotional needs met. You have a loud inner voice. To grow, you will have to learn to trust using it out loud.

The Abandoner: He divorced your mother, or your mother and father never married. He is unattainable and unavailable. You may not know where you stand with him at any given time. You may also feel you don't know who he is as a person.

(You) the Settler: You do not have an emotional relationship with your father, so you crave stability and believe that a "normal" relationship will make you feel whole. You settle anytime you can to avoid the pain of confronting your daddy dilemmas. You have rage just under the surface and do your best to not let it come roaring out. You vacillate between neediness and wanting to run. You have chameleon-like tendencies and have spent a lifetime learning how to fit into other people's lives. You want to stand on your own two feet but find it challenging to do so.

The Addict: Your dad is or was a drug user or an alcoholic. Whatever his addiction of choice, it made you grow up too fast. You became an adult at an early age because you had to parent your dad or possibly both of your parents.

(You) the Fixer: You are the mom in your relationships. You meet men who need to get their lives together. Somewhere in your subconscious, you believe if you could not fix your father, then by damn you will fix someone, but you keep choosing people who don't want to be fixed. Your love life is a series of self-fulfilling prophecies.

The Angel: Your dad passed away, and there will never be another man as perfect as he was. You want someone like him to love and protect you.

(You) the Independent: You miss your dad terribly and do not let men get to know the real you. You fear falling in love because you know it could be taken from you. You swing on a pendulum of falling head over heels quickly to warding off men altogether. You have a list of requirements a mile long and are determined not to settle. You want love but are not willing to be vulnerable enough to let someone into your life, because when you have, it has not worked out. Instead, you throw yourself into your career and busy yourself with everyone else's lives and problems. It is exhausting.

The Cheater: Your dad is unreliable. He may even be misogynistic. He cheated on your mother, leaving you to pick up the emotional pieces.

(You) Ms. Untrusting: You're not sure who you can trust, therefore you've had your heart broken a couple of times. You want to be in love and married but keep choosing guys who betray your trust. Angry about your track record, you don't understand why all men are jerks and why you can't just find one nice one. When you are in a relationship, you test your partner constantly, just waiting for him to show his true colors. Your emotions swing with the wind of his actions.

The Worker: Your dad either had a big-time career or a hobby that he valued more than his time with the family. He is a great provider financially but has no idea who you are emotionally. You secretly resent his career or hobby and want to be chosen by him or someone even if that someone bores you to tears.

(You) Ms. Needy: Whoever picks you, you will go with. You are the girl who always needs to have a man. The minute you break up with one, you are fixed up with the next. You don't give yourself any time to breathe, much less to understand who you are. You and Julia Roberts in *The Runaway Bride* have a lot in common, because you will do whatever it takes to fit into someone else's life to avoid being alone in your own.

Jackie was referred to me by Tanisha. Jackie had a strict upbringing with her mother and father. Her father was the Authoritarian type. Because her parents kept such close tabs on her growing up, never allowing her to fail, she was leading a life of safety versus one of free expression. By the time Jackie got to me, she was losing herself in every sense of the word. She was dating a man who was bisexual and had no idea. Jackie was not asking questions or seeking answers. She just knew she was unhappy, confused, and silent. Her upbringing was playing a significant role in her subconscious translation of who she was to be in relationships: seen and not heard. Because of her parents' coddling, Jackie had not been required to use her voice or think for herself. This essential lack of trial and error in young adulthood was causing her to flop in her adult relationships. She did not use her voice, and her backbone was like Silly Putty. Depression had set in, and she had no idea why or what to do. After we worked together for about six months, Jackie started to see the link between how she had been raised to feel and what she currently felt, which was completely numb.

As Jackie gained the knowledge and strength needed to confront her boyfriend, she also started to blossom with her newfound voice. She used the tools she had learned and eventually confronted Taylor about their relationship and lack of intimacy. After many nights of crying, Taylor admitted his true sexuality to himself and Jackie. They called it quits and remain the best of friends today. Jackie is now in culinary school and dating the owner of a hip new restaurant in Chicago. She is exploring all of her options and learning to trust herself to make her own decisions. Taylor just introduced her to his new boyfriend. Today they both are at peace and consider their relationship breakdown as their coming-out party.

Here is a snapshot of a father's role in our lives:

- He teaches us to take risks, or not. Studies have shown that our ability to take chances come from cues from our fathers.
- He plays a role in our self-esteem. According to the section, "Fathers and Their Impact on Children's Well-Being" in the 2006 report "The Importance of Fathers in the Healthy Development of Children,"[1] a dad's impact on a child's self-esteem is huge. An involved father helps

---

1   Jeffrey Rosenberg and W. Bradford Wilcox, "The Importance of Fathers in the Healthy Development of Children," Child Abuse and Neglect User Manual Series, 2006, https://www.childwelfare.gov/pubPDFs/fatherhood.pdf.

a child have the confidence to explore and have good social connections.

- He shows us what it means to persevere. Randal Day, a professor at Brigham Young University's School of Family Life, says that when fathers have an authoritative parenting style, it has a direct impact on how children perceives themselves and how persistent they may be in their lives.
- He shows us how women should be treated through how he treats our mothers.

Here's the thing most of you need to know: The right relationship for you is out there, whether your father is a saint or has some issues. Understanding his role in your life will continue to give you a broader view of yourself and how your relationship locator works. The relationship you are currently stuck in or may have seemingly been broken by is just a speed bump. It will not be the only love you ever have. It is or was the love you were ready for at the time. My job is all about giving you perspective on your life and your growing concept of love. The more insight you have on your inner workings, the more you will grow and evolve in your future relationships. Your narrative is shifting as we speak.

YOUR MOM'S TYPE

Your father's type is only half of the story. Your mother also plays a valuable role in how you view and experience love.

When I think of my mother, a great big smile comes over my face. She was fiercely loyal, loving beyond words, and did not take any BS. My mother was the quintessential momma bear. Divorced in her late twenties and widowed by her mid-thirties, she had to go it alone with two small kids. Although we experienced a lot of trauma as a family unit, my mother made sure that we always found something to laugh about. I remember watching my mom, all of five-foot-one, dance around our house to "Hot Legs" by Rod Stewart. One of her signature moves was to grab the two refrigerator doors to hang on to and twist her hips while shimmying into a semisquat before popping back up and kicking her leg out right on cue to the line "I love you, honey!"

She was and still is my biggest supporter, my best friend, and my most prominent teacher. On the flip side of that, growing up without a father in the house was difficult on many levels. My mother had to play both parts and, as any parent will tell you, there are some things she would have done differently. Now, because I have done so much research into parenting roles and how they play out in our adult lives, I can understand many of her decisions. I know what she was trying to accomplish, and I would say that for all intents and purposes, she did an excellent job; however, her relationship issues and the ones her lineage instilled in her were also instilled in me. I have had to decipher many verbal and nonverbal cues. In my subconscious, I was scared to be alone. I also always felt like the bottom was going to drop out financially, because it had and it continued to do so throughout my childhood. As a result, I developed a tough-as-nails exterior, but inside I was shaking in my boots when it came to love.

As mentioned, I chose men whom I could leave but would never leave me, just as my mom's relationship locator had imprinted on me. What I have learned along the way is to embrace my feminine energy and tone down my male energy a tad. I don't have to always do everything all by myself. I have a loving partner who is ready, willing, and able to help me carry the load and celebrate the wins.

Think about your mother-daughter relationship. What is it like today? How was it growing up? Did you respect her? Did you agree with her choices? Are there things you would have done differently? A mother is the central role model in her daughter's life. By watching our mothers, we subconsciously take in how she views herself, carries herself, and what she thinks of herself. Then each of us, in turn, becomes a little mini-me. In fact, a study published in the *Journal of Neuroscience* found that mother-daughter relationships are the absolute strongest of all parent-child bonds when it comes to common ways their brains are wired to process emotion.[2]

> *"A mother is she who can take the place of all others but whose place no one else can take." —Cardinal Gaspard Mermillod*

Here is a snapshot of a mother's role:

- She teaches us empathy. She can relate to what we are going through because she can put herself in our shoes. Science has confirmed that.
- She teaches us that it is okay to lean on others and when to ask for help.
- She teaches us to love and value ourselves, and to love and value others.
- She shows us independence.
- She teaches us that it is okay to feel our emotions and express how we feel.

Some women may have had a less-than-ideal mother-daughter relationship. If your emotional needs were somehow not met

---

2   Jordana Cepelewicz, "Like Mother, Like Daughter—the Science Says So, Too," *Scientific American,* January 26, 2016, https://www.scientificamerican.com/article/like-mother-like-daughter-the-science-says-so-too/.

in childhood by your mother or father, you might be more susceptible to misreading signs in relationships and to building unhealthy styles of attachment to them. If you are fortunate enough to have had a positive nuclear family relationship, you probably grew up feeling supported and loved. You feel secure to make choices and have confidence in your feelings and emotions. A person whose emotional needs were not met in childhood may attach too early or frequently to a fairy-tale ideal of love and mistake control, abuse, or manipulation with love—and may have defunct coping mechanisms that cannot be sustained in adulthood. We will discuss this in more detail in an upcoming chapter.

I write all of this not to be a Debbie Downer but to give you insight into why you may be picking certain relationships. Identifying your mother type will continue to help you unfold who you are and how you are in relationships. Pick up that highlighter and identify your mother type. Again, you may see her in a few of these.

Who's Your Momma?

The Single Mother: She struggled to make it all work, so in turn, everyone struggled.

You: You learned to take on everything, and you may even pick up a few strays here and there. You want to ask for help but may not know how, or may not believe you can trust someone else to get things done.

The Nonsharer: She is a perfectionist and wants everyone to see just how exemplary her life is. Everything is in order, from her kids to her spice rack.

You: You don't like to be vulnerable. You are proud of your track record, and any chink in your armor could be detrimental to your psyche for fear of being judged. Therefore, you keep every problem to yourself, which can leave you feeling lonely or isolated when someone falls short.

Cassie, 31

I married what I thought was a wonderful man about seven years ago. Kevin is a stockbroker in NYC, or should I say *was* a stockbroker because now he is living on our sofa unemployed. We had a fast life for many years. He worked insane hours, which did not bother me much while I finished medical school. I found out he had cheated on me about the same time I found out his debt was upwards of three hundred thousand dollars. Combined with my school loans, we are in way over our heads.

My dad is my best friend. He said he could sense something was going on last time he and my mom came to visit us for the weekend. He called me the other day to ask what was going on. I did not want to tell him. I did not want him, or especially my mom, to know what a failure my marriage has become. Kevin never gets off the sofa. He swears the girl in his office was just a one-time thing. I want so badly to believe him. I don't know. I haven't told any of my friends, and I am not telling my parents unless I know for sure it is over. I am hurting so bad. I wish he would get his act together.

When Cassie shared this story with me, I felt so deeply for her. She learned to keep things private by watching her mother suffer alone. Cassie has friends, and I am sure a few of them would love to help her through this process. She just won't let them in. Many women who grew up with a mother who is a perfectionist go on to expect the same of themselves. For Cassie, the single act of unveiling her vulnerabilities would help her grow by leaps and bounds. She has tried everything from deep-breathing exercises to CBD oil, yet she is still wound up so tightly that one day soon she may implode. I asked her, "Do you really want to be married to Kevin, or is the fear of failure keeping you locked in?"

> **The Born-to-Be-a-Mom Mother:** She does anything and everything for you and even your friends. She washes your clothes, cooks for you, and continues to spoil you rotten even though you have long since left her house.

> **(You):** You like being taken care of and may ward off change. You may be more of the taker in relationships than the giver.

> **The Chameleon:** This mom does not like to take the lead or be center stage. She is inclined to do whatever her partner wants when it comes to parenting, where to take vacations, or what she wants for dinner. She either lacks an opinion or does not use her voice in the world.

> **(You):** Have you followed her lead? You may keep to yourself in relationships for fear of causing any drama, and you probably settle easily and quickly. Make sure you don't just fall in love

with love. Take the time to get to know yourself and your likes and dislikes before you take on someone else's entire life. You are the rock star; the other person may be the opening act.

The Mom Who Wishes She'd Had a Different Life: I know; "ouch" is right. To put it politely, this mom is negative. She projects all of her issues on her kids or blames them for the choices she felt she had to make. You sometimes wonder if she should have even had children.

(You): You keep to yourself and may not be open to your maternal side. You keep your life simple and drama-free. And because of your programming, you may be missing out on an utterly wonderful man. You have a strict list of expectations that may be hard to meet.

The Overachiever: She goes after all her dreams and is inspired by everything. She follows all of the fads and aspires to be great at everything.

(You): You may tire just watching her or by trying to be like her. You feel left out and like you aren't as cool as your own mom. You may look for an abundance of emotional support or cheerleading in your relationships.

The Late Bloomer: Your mom is in her second act of life. She is acting like a different person than she was in your childhood.

(You): You may be embarrassed and feel like you two have changed roles, or you are down with some of it but really you want your mom back. Either way, you question your foundation and wonder if you should explore more even though the right guy may be right in front of you.

The Protector: This mom is part badass and part meddler. She worries about you so much that she feels she has to take the lead sometimes in your personal business.

(You): You can handle your own business but sometimes question your choices. You don't completely trust yourself and can be hot and cold in your stances, which may confuse the people in your life.

In looking back at all of this, I know why Facebook put "It's complicated" as a choice for relationship status on its site. Relationships are not about just us. We carry our childhood experiences and baggage along for the ride. Now that you have identified your mother's and father's types, it is time to look at what is working for you and what is not. What vibe are you giving off? Have you turned into your mother, or are you possibly looking for your father? I am not here to say that those are the only two routes you can take. I am living proof of that. What I am asking you to do is hit the pause button to see what you want to take with you and whom you are ready to discard. Use that trusty relationship council to help you out here.

EXERCISE: IDENTIFY YOUR PARENTS' TYPES

Fill in the blanks.

My mother's type is

_____.

Three ways her type shows up in my life:
  1.
  2.
  3.

My father's type is

_____.

Three ways his type shows up in my life:
  1.
  2.
  3.

My answers would look something like this: My mother's type is the Single Mother. Her type shows up in my life in that I don't like to ask for help. I still worry about money and take the safe route to forgo issues. My father's type is the Abandoner and Fun Dad. Because of his loss and our emotional disconnect, I chose safety over love. I took my power back when I decided to stop settling and got on with figuring out what I wanted out of life.

I am so pumped that you are on this journey with me. We have covered a great deal so far. You are making real changes with each chapter. Thank you for trusting me and my process. You are getting closer and closer to the life you want. Believe that it can happen. By participating in this journey, you are setting the intention to change your narrative and change your life. The power lies in your intention. Your intention dictates your direction, and your direction leads you to your destiny.

CHAPTER 5

WHO'S THE GUY?
BAD BOYS, COMMITMENTPHOBES,
AND OTHER DUDES WHO
DON'T DESERVE YOU

"*I*t is with hearts full of sadness that we have decided to separate. We have conducted our relationship privately, and we hope that as we consciously uncouple and co-parent, we will be able to continue in the same manner."

Do you remember when Gwyneth Paltrow and Chris Martin put out this statement about their breakup? Along with the statement, Gwyneth's Goop website posted information about "conscious uncoupling" in an article written by her mentor, Doctor Habib Sadeghi. Gwyneth went on to talk in the media about divorce and said, "What if the divorce itself is not the problem? What if it is a symptom of something deeper that needs our attention?"

Statistics today show that over half of marriages end in divorce. I, along with Gwyneth, feel that divorces are caused by something deeper. To go a step further, I also believe that any heartbreak you experience is an indicator of something deeper that needs to be healed. As human beings, we continue to manifest scenarios that will repair those parts of ourselves that are keeping us from the purest form of love we are meant to have. Love within ourselves has to be present before we can ever give love to another. It is time to take a serious look at yourself. Are you picking men out of learned patterns subconsciously, or are you consciously coupling?

The message that we are lovable and meant for something worthy can take many heartbreaks and sleepless nights to sink in if we have been programmed to think or believe otherwise. It is difficult to understand when our own decisions take over and when those learned messages take a back seat.

The reason women get stuck on a particular guy is that these two worlds of past and present collide. When this happens, there is a disjunction between what her head is telling her and what her heart is demanding. It is as though she is walking through her life with someone else dictating every turn she makes. The guy is her salvation, the one she has decided on, even if there are red flags on every corner. She has quit listening to her instincts and is using sheer determination. The high their relationship is giving her tells her heart that he is her guy, even if her relationship council and family see otherwise.

This is where the mirror starts to come into focus. She may begin to ask herself questions like, "What do I want? Is love supposed to be this hard?" She is starting to look for answers. She begins to believe she is worth it, but is the guy worth it?

No, love is not supposed to be that hard. Sure, some obstacles arise in our relationships, but they should make us stronger, not weaker. Love is clearly defined in the Oxford dictionary as "an intense feeling of deep affection, a great interest, and pleasure in something." Nowhere does it mention pain.

You are here because something is broken—either your belief in yourself or your faith in love. You need to understand whom you are choosing and why. The reason you have gotten to this place is apparent: programming. You have forgotten what "normal" looks like or may have never even seen an example of a healthy, normal relationship in your own family.

Let's explore the types of guys you may date and what their behaviors look like in the real world. We'll examine what a guy's behavior might look like and how you might (subconsciously) respond to him because of the programming that has been wired into you by your family of origin.

THE MIRROR EFFECT

Take a pen and place a check mark by any of the guy types below that you have fallen for or may be in deep mourning over currently. There is no judgment here. I, too, have fallen hard for a guy whom I should not have given so much of my time and headspace to; however, I can tell you that it was because of my relationship with him that *I* finally came into focus. I like to call this phenomenon the mirror effect.

The mirror effect happens the moment you shift your attention from the guy or the situation and back to yourself. You are ready to look at yourself in the mirror and see all of your beautiful flaws, and this man who broke your heart has given you a gift— the gift of self-actualization.

You have been hurt enough that it is time to wave the white flag. You want help, so I am going to take you for a walk down memory lane to look at some of the men you may have loved before or are currently considering. This will be a cheat sheet for which guys to avoid.

As you read through the list, it is crucial to focus on your subconscious translations—a translation you make that you are not fully aware of, but it influences your actions and feelings. It happens in your unconscious. It happens to us in our formative years as we watch our parents navigate their romantic relationships. As you read about these types of guys, go back to your relationship history and try to write down the subconscious translation you learned in childhood that defines your relationship with that person. I must warn you, this is like drinking a truth serum. It is that good.

I am bringing the guys to avoid into focus because you may have on rose-colored glasses when it comes to some of them. As you read through my list, think about what some of your ex-lovers have in common. Do you see a pattern? Have you been choosing the same types of guys and expecting a different result?

Guy types to avoid:

The Submarine: The new pop culture term for a man you are dating who ghosts you for no real reason, only to pop back up a few months later with no explanation or apology as to why he disappeared in the first place.

Do not fall for this one, ladies. He is confused and will only continue to be confused. This guy has no clue what he wants. He is always on the lookout for the next best thing. When he meets someone new (and perhaps, in his eyes, more interesting), he will disappear for some time. When the new one no longer piques his interest, he will suddenly remember you,

the perfect catch, and come back to find you.
Bottom line: If he does not value you from the
start, move on.

Macy fell in love with a Submarine. He was in his mid-for-ties when they met and was still running the streets. She was ten years his junior and completely smitten with him. The Sub would take her out on the obligatory Sunday night, or they would have a Netflix-and-chill-type date on a Monday or Tuesday. He wanted to save Wednesday through Sunday for his boys—so he could chase women half his age.

After I coached her a bit, Macy and I decided she would start declining his offers, which only made him work harder. He soon asked her out to a cookout on a Saturday night. But once he checked the box of a weekend date, he went right back to the Sunday–Tuesday dates.

Macy was confused. But when we started unpacking her childhood, we realized that Macy's mother and father had lived two separate lives in one loveless marriage. On the outside, they had it all. They never fought, and they kissed at the appropriate times, but where was the passion? Macy never saw it. Her sub-conscious translation was: In relationships, men do what they want. Women sometimes take what they can get.

Macy and I went on to work together for over a year. She learned her worth and put the Submarine on ice. He kept trying to win her back. She explained to him what she expected and did not wait around to see if he could deliver. Thankfully, he figured it out after Macy moved on with her life. He put in the work, and when Macy felt comfortable, she gave him a final chance. He passed with flying colors. Today they have a thriving marriage with twin daughters who are the apple of his eye.

The Cheater: This is the guy who never puts you first or makes you feel good enough. Somehow, he has manipulated you into believing that his cheating is your fault or something he could not avoid. Yes, people make mistakes; however, a commitment is a commitment. The person you are giving your all to should do the same. If he cheated once, you have a decision to make. Is he willing to take action to do whatever it takes (without blaming you at all) to work toward getting your trust back? Look at yourself closely here. Are you at your absolute best with him, or has he robbed you of your self-worth in any way? If he has made you feel "less than" or he is a serial cheater, *run!*

Cheaters are sneaky little scoundrels. Many times, they come across like the moral police in the beginning. They are quick to offer their support and also manipulate you into believing their core characteristics are made of steel. These guys come on strong and usually leave in a puff of disloyal smoke. An example of this is Willow's story.

Willow's college sweetheart, Craig, cheated on her with a dancer from a local men's club. She found out when a friend of Craig's, Todd, told her one night. Willow did the noble thing and put her boyfriend on ice. A few months after the breakup, Todd called to ask Willow out to dinner. He told her how much he liked her and reiterated what a player her ex was. Soon they started dating, and Willow told all of her friends what a great guy Todd was turning out to be.

About eight months in, Todd began acting up. He was staying out until all hours of the night and letting his phone run out of battery power while he was out. When Willow confronted Todd about his behavior, he flipped the script on her, saying she was too controlling. "No wonder Craig wanted a break," he yelled into the phone. Willow was hurt and started wondering if she was indeed the reason both guys reacted by being disrespectful. Her head was getting so discombobulated with the opinions of her friends and the reaction from Todd that she went against her better judgment. She relaxed on her expectations, and soon their relationship was in no man's land. Todd took full advantage of her being a doting girlfriend while he ran the streets on the weekends. One night everything changed. Willow ran into Craig at a party while she was out with some of her friends. He pulled her into a corner and told her that Todd was a scumbag and had been cheating on her with her friend Barbara behind her back.

If we rewind this story, we will see the moment Willow gave her power away. She relinquished it by letting someone else's needs come before her own. She had every right to ask the guy she was in a committed relationship with to check in while he was out. By his throwing up a roadblock from her past, she was thrown off her game and questioned her expectations in the relationship. For Willow, trust is one of the core characteristics she needs in a relationship. We will discuss these characteristics in a later chapter. For now, it is valuable for you to see what types of issues keep arising in your relationships. Are you conscious of your needs and your deal-breakers, or are you dating subconsciously?

The Commitmentphobe: This is the guy who can't seem to make a decision when it comes to your future with him. We have all heard the excuses men use to block the progression of a relationship, like "I need to get my career on track." (Translation: "My commitment is to the firm and not to you. If you don't mind being second or third fiddle, have at it.") Another good one is "Something is wrong with me. It's not you; it's me." (Translation: "I must be an idiot because I know you are an awesome girl. I don't want you.") Yes, this is a hard one to swallow, because for all intents and purposes he may look right on paper; however, he is not the guy for you.)

Ask yourself if his reasons have any validity. If your gut calls BS, believe it. Commitments should follow a standard sequence welcomed by both people. They should enrich the relationship, not cause upheaval. If you feel him tensing up when talk of the future comes up, it may be time to reevaluate what *you* want. Do you want him or just the commitment itself?

In full disclosure, my husband and I dated for eight years before we got married. There were a multitude of reasons why: timing, long distance, age, careers, opinions, and a few more. The one thing we always had was respect for and honesty with each other. I even dated another guy for a year and a half midway through. My husband was not a true commitmentphobe per se. I never questioned where I stood or his love for me. His lack of commitment to me was because he was committed to his career. I was second fiddle at times—like during basketball season.

Because I was deeply enmeshed in working on myself, the distance did not kill us. It gave us the room to grow individually. I did kick and scream ultimatums a few times, but they never panned out. The reason we have worked out is that we push each other to be a better person. Our timing eventually worked out. The message here is this: If you have a great guy who makes you feel loved, he may be worth the wait. You have to decide if what he is capable of giving is enough until you are both on the same page.

> **The Ghoster:** This guy comes on strong, only to leave faster than he came in. He loves to fall in love but has no interest in maintaining it, because he does not have the emotional tools or maturity to do the work. This guy is trouble because when a relationship hits too much of a snag, he will drop you like a bad habit and run. This uncertainty is sure to make you go crazy. In many ways, a relationship with this type can show you how you may have come off to others in your past relationships. He needs more help than you do, and you don't have time for all that.

> **The Breadcrumb Giver:** This guy is just flirty enough to make you think he is interested in you. He flirts but does not follow through. His hot-and-cold tendencies can make you question yourself. If you are not careful, you will put yourself in harm's way trying to get his attention in any way you can. Don't settle for a crumb— you deserve the entire loaf. He is a man-child and needs to go back to the playground. This guy wants to play. Leave him with the Legos.

Be careful with Breadcrumb Givers. These guys tend to lurk around when you are sick and tired of being out in the scene. They have this crazy radar and can find women like yourself who are ready to settle down in an instant. One of my friends talked about one of her Breadcrumb Givers for five years. Almost on cue, the minute she would become single she would run into Brian. He was this beautiful Adonis-looking guy who stood six foot four and had guns ablazing. He had come on strong the first time they met, telling her that she reminded him of his childhood sweetheart. He spent the night with her and asked her to accompany him to a wedding in Greece later that month. He called her nonstop for the next two or three days, then—*poof*—he was gone. A year or so later she ran into him at a street fair, where he apologized profusely, blaming his absence on a business deal gone wrong. They exchanged numbers, and he started pursuing her again. A week later, she cooked dinner for him, and they talked until the sun came up. He left and never called her afterward. A few years later she ran into him. Again, he told her how sorry he was, and this time asked if she wanted to accompany him to church that Sunday. They went to church and lunch at a hip new spot on the battery in Atlanta. They talked for hours and made plans for the next week. She even called him out on all of his ghosting, for which he took all of the blame. She never heard from him again.

What a waste of headspace this guy was. My friend is now happily married. As a side note, when she and her husband were looking for a lot to build a house on, they found one in Brookhaven, an affluent family neighborhood in Atlanta. It was for sale by the owner. You will never guess who the owner was. Yes, Brian. He was still single, beautiful, and just as distracted as ever.

> **The Cuffer:** This guy wants to settle down for the winter. He is like a bear in that all he wants to do is hibernate and get fed. These guys are notorious for leaving before Valentine's Day.

You can call him on his bluff by planning a summer trip and seeing if he commits. Many times, these guys do want love; however, they are stuck in between two worlds. They crave love and commitment and also want to play.

These relationships are not all bad. They have the possibility of leading somewhere. Just don't set up house with someone who does not want to have a future with you. You have to ask yourself how much time you are willing to waste to figure it out. As a side note, my ex (discussed in chapter two) was a partial Cuffer and, in the end, a full-blown commitmentphobe.

Women can be Cuffers, too. My client Mitsy has Cuffer tendencies. She is a stand-up comedian and has countless stories about dating. Most of her relationships have a failure-to-thrive tendency, which goes along nicely with her fear of commitment. We are working on her commitment issues and making significant progress. She has allowed me to share one of her Cuffer stories.

I met Jerry while in Kentucky for a gig. We had a wild weekend, and for a few weeks, he kept my mind off of Scott—Scott being "the guy" that will not fully commit to me. Scott and I were on a break when Jerry came into the picture. Jerry asked me to go away on a ski trip, all expenses paid, to North Carolina—a "low-rent" skiing trip, in my opinion, but I went anyway. I'm not turning down any free adventure, even if I might have to ski on sleet! The first night was great. On the second day, though, I was getting anxious.

I missed Scott, and Jerry had a few distracting qualities. For one, he did not pronounce his *l*s. He said stuff like "Super Bow" instead of "Super Bowl." I thought I had maybe not heard him correctly until he asked me if I was code instead of cold. I snuck into the bathroom and called a friend to discuss. She reminded me that I was single and should try and enjoy the rest of the weekend. By the next morning, we were snowed in. They were not letting anyone on the roads, and I had had enough. It was New Year's Day. I had decided the night before that I was tired of living like this and was ready to try and make it work with Scott. I was going to work Denna's process and get my life together in this new year, but first I had to get out of Snowmageddon.

As we waited for word on the roads, Jeff obliged me by watching a Hallmark movie. I lay down on the sofa and bundled up, just praying for the sun to do her magic. Jerry scooped my head up and laid it across his lap, playing with my hair and tickling my scalp. I was in a little slice of heaven—just with the wrong dude. I waited until I was about to pee in my pants to get up. When I came back in to reclaim my spot of the sofa, Jerry told me to have a seat beside him. He did a quick Houdini switch and sprawled his body out, placing his much-too-gelled head in my lap. He looked up at me and said, "I'm code [cold], too. Want to scratch my head now?" At that moment, I regretted the entire thing. I did not want to be there any longer. Period. I said,

"I can't. I have an aversion to scalps!" What a piece of work I am.

Believe it or not, Mitsy made it out of Snowmageddon. She and Scott finally moved to the same city and are living together "in sin." Her words, not mine.

> **The Bencher:** This guy puts you on ice anytime he wants to go play. He will never let you go entirely, in case he decides he wants you on his team. These guys are usually cheaters. When they have the chance to roam, they take it.
>
> Make sure your feelings matter. Does he include you in his trips? Does he take you along when he is with his friends? Does his family know about you? If you are feeling insecure about his level of long-term interest, it may be time to find another starter.

> **The Jerk:** This guy makes you feel bad about yourself. He is critical of you, your friends, or your family. If anyone makes you feel bad about yourself even once, it is too often. Mental, physical, or verbal abuse is a deal-breaker. Tell a friend you trust. Confide it all. If your relationship council sees a red flag, it is probably time to walk away.

Gerri had dated a few Jerks. I first met her when she called in to my show, "Keeping It Real with Denna, the Girlfriend Guru." She called in a lot, so we had become friends in the digital age. Gerri is an Accommodator type, so she tends to let a guy slide despite some pretty major red flags.

She spent the better part of a year and a half with a Jerk who did a number on her. When they met, he had a girlfriend, but that did not stop him from putting on the full-court press with Gerri. When she relented and started dating him, he told her about this ex of his who still had clothes and furniture at his house that she needed to pick up.

Gerri called in and asked me how to handle it.

My advice was to let her guy handle it. If the guy and his ex were broken up, she should want to get her stuff and get on with her life in a timely matter. A month later, his ex had come by twice, taking only a few things at a time. Oh, and by the way, they still texted weekly.

I encouraged Gerri to put him on ice until he could make a clean break.

You guessed it. She did not follow my advice.

They continued to fight a lot, and Gerri, being an Accommodator, just kept hoping for the best, never asserting her wants or needs. About a year into their relationship, he confided that his ex needed to move back in due to financial issues. Believe it or not, Gerri went along with it. The guy told her it would be for only a few weeks and said he loved her for understanding his just wanting to help out an old friend. The next day she caught them in bed together.

I share Gerri's story with you to remind you that we all stumble across a Jerk or two in our lives. The lesson is to learn from the situation to trust your instincts. Deep down, Gerri is still questioning her worth. She desperately wants to both give and receive love. But at what cost?

Her family of origin dealt with a lot of mental illness. She learned to be accommodating because she had to be. Her father was a surgeon, and her mother was bipolar, in and out of institutions. When her mother was away for treatment, sometimes for many months at a time, Gerri would be shipped off to her aunt and uncle's house. They had four kids of their own, so Gerri just had to fit in where she could. Subconscious translation: Hope for the best. Don't make waves. Get love when and where you can.

If you are guilty of dating or falling in love with any of these types, consider yourself normal. It is what you do after you identify this that will make the difference. You need to let the bad one go to make room in your life for the good one.

If you are with Mr. Right Now, you don't have a prayer of finding Mr. Right for You. It takes a lot of energy to try to keep alive a relationship that is going nowhere. Not everyone is long-term material. By identifying some of the types of men you have chosen, you should start to see some patterns in your relationship history.

EXERCISE: RED LIGHT, GREEN LIGHT

I am continuing with the theme of how childhood patterns and translations may be precluding you from knowing the telltale signs that something is off and what to do about it. This will help you navigate any landmines you may face when you get back out there.

Pull out your trusty journal. Write down any red-light or green-light characteristics each lover had on the open page beside his name.

Red-light characteristics (don't walk; run away):

> Treats you or others disrespectfully
> Is dishonest and makes you question his intentions
> Does not bring you around friends or family

Has anger toward his ex that seems bigger or lasts longer
than the situation warrants
Does not do what he says he is going to do
Has financial distress
Makes you feel insecure in any way with words or actions
Cannot resolve an issue in a healthy manner

Green-light characteristics (indicating long-term potential):

You feel excited about where the relationship is going
You feel proud of who he is and how he treats you
He lets you feel vulnerable
He accepts you for you
Your family and friends approve
You can ultimately be yourself (Spanx or no Spanx)
You can be honest about your feelings
Your disagreements bring your closer

Hopefully, you are starting to get into your groove here. By now, some of your patterns are beginning to take shape, and you are beginning to understand what does and does not work for you. We will continue to discuss patterns in relationships in the next chapter. Remember this: You are loved and lovable. Every single day in my work, I see women who think they will never get the love they want or deserve. My process works. I have watched it hundreds and hundreds of times yield positive results. Love is out there. Right now, you are just taking a little bit of time to get your game face on.

PART II:
UNWRAPPING THE PRESENT

CHAPTER 6

RELATIONSHIP PATTERNS: WHEN THE PAST INTRUDES ON PRESENT RELATIONSHIPS

*I*n Dani Shapiro's book *Inheritance*, she unfolds her personal story of how she figured out the man she thought was her biological father was not, after she received her DNA results from Ancestry.com. She marvels at how she would look closely at the mirror as a child to try to find traces of her nonbiological father in her face before she even knew the truth. There was something inside of her, a little bell, trying to warn her that things were not as they seemed. In the mirror, she looked for truth.

At fifty-three years old, she finally met her biological father for the first time. She studied him and saw so much of herself in him—features, mannerisms, and physical similarities. Although the meeting with her biological father filled in so many of the blanks for her, her connection and dedication to the man she called her father remained undeniable. He had taught her how to love, and their shared experiences were woven into who she was, how she loved, and how she received love. His emotional imprint had made her the woman she was, although another man's DNA had given her the gift of life. The book goes on to share the odyssey of nature versus nurture and what makes us who we are. It begs the question, are we defined by our genealogy or by a combination of biology, experiences, and learned behaviors?

I GOT IT FROM MY MOMMA!

Though we are all unique, we still carry the lineage of our parents. We want to see ourselves in our parents and know where we came from, but we also want to know that we can lead different lives. There are parts we get from our parents that we cherish, like our mother's great smile or our father's sense of humor; however, as with all humans, there are also flaws. We take not only their DNA but their learned experiences in the world. We see how they have maneuvered the ups and downs in their lives, and before we even know it, we are mirroring those same behaviors in our own lives. These mirrored behaviors are called coping mechanisms.

A coping mechanism is what we use to adapt to environmental stressors, based on conscious or unconscious choices that enhance our control over the behavior or give us physical comfort. How you dealt with stress as a child and how you deal with stress as an adult are two different animals. Things that may have worked in your younger years before you had the tools or emotional maturity to handle conflict may no longer work for you as an adult. For example, if when you were seven or eight years old your parents told you that you could not go to a birthday party, you may have attempted to cope by storming off to your room. Now, as an adult, if your partner tells you he does not want you to attend a gathering with him, stomping off or running to your room may be seen as a futile or immature way of coping. Just like triggers, coping mechanisms are tied to our childhood experiences.

THE IN-BETWEEN STAGE

Believe it or not, your coping mechanisms have played a big part in where you are today in the love department. You are stuck in the in-between stage. You don't know whether to go or stay in a current relationship, or perhaps there is an old love you can't seem to shake. You feel like you played a part in the demise of the relationship, and you want to either go back and fix it or stay alone and fix yourself. It can be an unnecessary evil, getting stuck in the in-between stage of your love timeline. The beginning of the in-between stage can feel like purgatory, because your thoughts are in a constant loop with you wondering if you should go back and give the relationship another chance.

As women, we usually get stuck in the in-between time during a monumental shift in who we are becoming. We may want to go back to an old love but feel a shift in how we would go about it. Because the change is active, we are not completely clear which side we want to take. This time in our process is paramount for the building of who we want to become. If we go back, we go back to the old coping mechanisms or ways that no longer serve a purpose in our lives. The minute we concede, the clock starts ticking. We go back to an unhealthy relationship or one we have outgrown, and it blows up in our face like a preset bomb. All of the things we can no longer avoid smack us right in the face, because once we have begun to make a shift, we can no longer sit in relationship limbo. The new self is dying to come out. Thus, the old relationship patterns won't do anymore.

When you can no longer deal with an old situation, you are in the in-between phase. You know you don't want to go back, but you are scared to move forward. Moving on requires growth, and growth means leaving some people behind. During this middle stage, you have to push yourself ahead always. Many times, it requires shedding your old life to make room for the new one. Old friends may not like the new you. You are starting to represent freedom, and that scares people. By changing, you may require the people around you also to shift and grow. Not everyone will be ready to see the transformation.

The end of the in-between stage is where all the fun takes place. I like to call it a training ground. It is when you try out new coping skills, and boundaries start to find their way to the forefront. We will discuss boundaries at length in an upcoming chapter. The end of the in-between stage is where the narrative shift begins to come to center stage. You are letting go of what no longer serves you and replacing it with the narrative that better suits your desire to take your relationship power back. Your old coping mechanisms helped you survive. They did their job, but now you are ready for the big league. You are prepared to evolve to get what it is you are looking for.

To get real clarity around what has gotten you to where you are, we need to take one last look at where you have been in the coping pond and how your parents have played a part in the whole thing.

YOU GROW, GIRL!

Maybe you swore that you would never have a relationship like your parents'; perhaps you swore you wouldn't be happy unless you found a relationship just like your parents'. You may be here because you have not achieved either and are stuck! Those parental patterns are hard to break, and now you have learned that some robust programming has taken place in your past.

There is an intrinsic pull to the familiar, so if you come from a family of huggers and you are with people who shake hands instead, you might feel uncomfortable. But when you meet up with people who wrap you in a bear hug upon first meeting, it can feel like home. The problem comes when the familiar is not so healthy—like abuse, disrespect, or ignoring. That can feel familiar, too, and it may be why you have gravitated, without really realizing it, to someone who operates just like dear old Mom or Dad.

Without knowing it, your parents' dysfunction can creep into your adult relationships. Patterns can persist unless they are looked at and broken down. These patterns are what set in motion coping mechanisms, both healthy and unhealthy. How we cope, learned to cope, or don't cope can have a lasting effect on our relationships. Lack of coping yields to the blurring of boundaries, and the cycle continues. We go right back to what we know. We don't grow, and you are here to grow, girl!

EXERCISE: RELATIONSHIP AWARENESS

In this relationship awareness exercise, you will write it all out.

1. Write your parents' love story.
   - What was the main conflict?
   - What were/are each parent's hallmark coping mechanisms?
2. Write your own relationship story of "the guy."
   - What were/are your trademark coping mechanisms?
   - What were/are his?

Yes, we are about to get into the crux of it all. Do some research: Ask your mother and father about what drew them to each other. (If they are not available to ask, ask someone who witnessed their relationship, or just try to do your best.) What were they running from or to?

What did they think the other had to offer?
What were/are the overarching issues in their relationship?
If their relationship did not work out, why not?
What coping mechanisms may have hindered their
    communication?
Is there any unfinished business?
Who needs to forgive?
Who needs to move on?

Ask yourself all of the same questions, too. Are there any recurring themes? Do you see any similarities? If so, highlight the themes in your stories. There is no right or wrong answer here. This exercise is all about discovery. What you need to know will be revealed. Trust the process.

EXERCISE: IDENTIFY YOUR COPING MECHANISMS

Now that you know your history, let's dig a little deeper into how you cope in times of frustration. Let's identify what you have learned that works and what needs to be discarded. Here is a list of possible learned coping mechanisms. Highlight any that you identify with. Put a star beside any you identify with through your parents' actions.

Unhealthy coping mechanisms:

Isolation—not answering the phone or declining invitations

Physical or verbal lashing out—fighting physically or verbally

Mentally shutting down—sleeping too much or crying incessantly

Passive-aggressive behaviors—lashing out indirectly with the intent to cause strife

Neediness—not wanting to be alone and expecting others to comfort you to avoid coping on your own

Social media stalking—using social media to take jabs at, stalk, or check up on people

Sexual avoidance or aggressiveness—using sex as a means of coping or abstaining entirely

Addictive behaviors—using alcohol or drugs, including prescription drugs (self-medicating), to check out emotionally

Bulimia, anorexia, or overeating—using food to avoid feelings or not eating to gain control when you feel out of control

Shopping—numbing yourself through the high of spending money, although you may not be able to afford your purchases

Self-blame loop—using thoughts of blame as a way of self-harming

OCD traits—overcleaning, ritual behaviors, or overexercising

Going back to an unhealthy ex-boyfriend—another form of impulsivity to avoid doing the work needed to move on

Gambling—another way of self-numbing through compulsive acts

I am sure you can pick out a few of these coping mechanisms and attach them to your family. Depending on your generation and the generation of your parents, your styles may differ. In my parents' generation, there was no Doctor Phil or an entire aisle in the bookstore dedicated to self-help. For them, getting through it meant just living through it. Dealing with an issue meant not dealing with it, and many times maladaptive coping mechanisms came into play.

My generation is the first that wants to put our issues on blast. We no longer wish to suffer in silence. For us, hitting our issues head-on is the way we choose to deal. You are going to want to get your parents or stand-in parents involved in your relationship transformation. Understanding why they did what they did to cope will help you see why you may do what you do.

I remember when I first went to therapy to deal with my father-related abandonment issues. The therapist brought up all kinds of issues that I had yet to deal with and resolve. I started to see that my family had attempted to deal with things by avoiding the hard topics. In doing so, my father had coped by drinking and my mother had coped with food. I had wrestled with different coping mechanisms but settled on isolation, which I would later find out while doing research for my book *The Fatherless Daughter Project* was the hallmark coping mechanism of a fatherless daughter. Isolation worked for me because I had learned avoidance from my parents. I thought that by isolating myself, I was coping. I was dipping out long enough to either dust myself off or wait for someone to rescue me. "The guy" I chose to give my all to had nothing to give back, and it was only when I wanted out of isolation and back into the population that my process was born. Today I use many of the positive coping mechanisms listed below to deal with my issues head-on. Of course, I still love a chocolate milkshake, but because I have done the work, I completely understand how and why I do the things I do.

Healthy coping mechanisms:

Facing issues head-on in a conversation—healthy conflict yields resolution

Enforcing healthy boundaries—knowing and enforcing how you are treated and treat others

Engaging in physical activity—releases dopamine (a feel-good brain chemical)

Listening to music—releases feel-good endorphins and stimulates the brain

Finding humor—laughing is always the best medicine

Asking for space while you get perspective on a situation—shows emotional maturity; you know how to take the time needed to understand your actions and reactions to situations

Journaling—writing is a healthy way of processing and understanding emotions

Having a spiritual practice—gaining perspective and feeling as though you are a part of something bigger helps with self-love

Letting go of the small stuff—deciding to let go of things that do not matter in the big picture is empowering

Self-help—taking the time and effort to heal through introspection

Seeking a mentor—learning how someone else got to where he or she wanted to be is a big step in getting your power back through action

Seeking a coach—having another person's perspective on your life can work wonders

Therapy—working on past issues and traumas can help you better understand yourself and how you relate to others

Travel—seeing new things and discovering new places reminds us there is more to life out there

I have seen so many of my clients go on to find not just love but their life's purpose on this journey. The in-between stage is the perfect time to start getting bold. You may not be ready for partnership, but you can begin to have a little fun while you are figuring it all out. Don't be afraid to take a trip, get a coach, or try some therapy.

One of the best things I did in the in-between stage was raise money for the Leukemia & Lymphoma Society with its Team in Training. I needed something to occupy my time while I was still in love with a guy, in a relationship that would eventually lead to nowhere. I was working on myself in the hope of either getting over him or healing toward him. I decided that I might as well get in shape while I did something for others, so I signed up with the Team in Training for the San Diego marathon. I grabbed a friend who was also in an in-between time. We got busy raising money and raising our vibrations, and while my body was becoming stronger, so was my mind. With every hardearned mile, I gained more and more answers. I was starting to see how I had become me. I was gathering information from my mother along the way, and with each story shared, she and I were beginning to heal.

A few months into my training, I went out with a group of friends. A tall, good-looking guy walked past me, and for the first time in almost two years, I felt something for someone else other than "the guy." His name was Jon, and years later, he would become my husband.

A few years ago, I was doing research for a talk I would be giving on trauma, and came across a study from 1980 by two psychologists at the University of North Carolina who discovered that trauma changes people in four compelling ways:

1. It gives them inner strength.
2. It brings them closer to family and friends.
3. It brings more meaning to their lives.

4. It can be the catalyst for changing their lives and finding purpose.

All four of those things happened on my journey toward taking my power back in my dating relationships. I found inner strength when I allowed myself the room to heal. My family and I became closer as I dug deeper into my past, enabling all of us to open up the lines of communication that had been buried long before. I found meaning in my life as a writer, healer, mother, and wife. And through it all, I found my purpose in helping people take their power back in their lives. Now, I am not saying you have to go out and run a marathon. Nevertheless, I am empowering you to start thinking of what positive coping mechanisms you can slowly incorporate into your life, starting today.

BLURRED LINES

Some coping mechanisms ride the fence. Some of them can be both healthy and unhealthy, depending on how they are put to use. For an entire year after my infamous breakup, I survived on Jake's Chocolate Slap Yo Mama milkshakes. Jake's ice cream made the lonely weeks and months in Breakupville more tolerable. Of course, an exercise in moderation may have been a healthier way to cope with the stress, but at the time, I just wanted the comfort of those milkshakes. The marathon would come later.

Today, I see so many people choosing to work themselves into the ground as a coping mechanism, because being "too busy" has become acceptable. I am currently working with a couple who are both "too busy" as a way of refusing to work on their genuine issues. They love each other dearly, but intimacy is the issue. Yes, they have sex—just not often enough. They have four kids, so on the outside, it makes sense that they are running around like two chickens with their heads cut off; however, they want to slow down. They miss each other. They both learned to overwork to check out from the marriage and its responsibilities. They are at a crossroads in their marriage and want off the fast track. We are working together to wean them from their lifestyle and get them back to what makes them happy: each other.

Another blurred line in coping is when the coping mechanism is not necessarily detrimental but can be misleading. Take Michelle, a client I worked with who was beyond frustrated with her inability to find love. When we got to this part of the process, she got stumped, and her eyes brimmed with tears. She said, "I cry over everything. I always have. It is just what I do." Upon digging further, she had the revelation that she used tears as her go-to coping mechanism, yet when I asked her how that was working for her, she could not answer. We traced her tears back to her mother. Michelle said that when she herself was growing up, her mother would cry if she was mad, happy, or sad. "She was not coping at all—just crying," Michelle said after I pointed out that her attempts to cope were a replica of her mother's.

Later, in one very poignant exchange between Michelle and her twelve-year-old daughter, Michelle learned the impact of her unhealthy coping mechanisms on her daughter. Her daughter, a wise soul, noticed that Michelle was having a sciatica flare-up as a reaction to a disagreement she'd had with her boyfriend. She said, "Mommy, I think working with Denna is helping." Michelle, amused, asked, "Why would you say that?" To that, her daughter replied, "Well you didn't run to your room and cry today. I know you were sad, but we still got to have dinner together." Talk about a heart punch. This work is real. Think about the reactions you have to your emotional distress. Are you coping or finding ways not to cope at all? Look at your learned behaviors and who is on the receiving end of them. It may be time to throw out the old and bring in the new.

EXERCISE: IDENTIFY YOUR COPING MECHANISM

To bring it all together, fill in the blanks to this sentence. You may even want to try to do this exercise for your parents, too.

I get triggered when

_____.

I react by

_____.

My default coping mechanism is

_____.

A few ways I will try to positively cope moving forward are

_____,

_____,

_____.

So, in Michelle's case, she would have said, "I get triggered when I don't get my way or enough attention from [person's name]. I react by becoming needy. My default coping mechanism is to cry and shut down. I will start incorporating listening to music and exercising to help me bring in some of those feel-good endorphins."

Michelle has also added a psychotherapist to the mix. She is determined to take her power back in all aspects of her life moving forward. She finally sees that everything is connected. The emotional issues we refuse to deal with affect us spiritually, emotionally, and physically. In her case, the crying and sciatica flare-ups proved to be old-fashioned ways of coping long-term.

As Michelle discovered, the more we try to hold it all, the more likely it is that our emotions will find a negative way out. Think of your mind, body, and soul alignments. What is out of sync and why? What feeling are you holding in or holding back that is causing the rest of your life to veer off track? Is it coming out in you physically, as with Michelle, or emotionally in avoidance or outbursts toward others? Are you suffering spiritually, looking for something more prominent in your life, like purpose? Only you know the answers. I hope by exploring your past and taking part in this process, you are starting to see the changes that need to be made. There is no time like the present.

RELATIONSHIP RESCUE

Let me let you in on a little secret. We all want to be rescued. Many of the relationships that we enter into are for some form of being rescued, and I don't always mean damsel in distress. We are either running toward something/someone or away from something/someone. We may be running from boredom and looking for someone exciting to take the lead in our lives. Maybe you are a single mother and running toward a partner who can help you bear the load. Perhaps you have played it safe for far too long, and you want to be rescued from the monotony and whisked into the unbelievable. Perchance your biological clock is ticking, and you are looking to be rescued from the chance of ending up childless, so you latch on to the best person in the moment. Whatever it is, we are all looking for love. We want it so much that sometimes we jump at the first thing that comes our way.

We want to fill the void of whatever has been eluding us, so we strike while the iron is hot because damn it, we deserve it! It happens so frequently that I coined the phrase "relationship reality" as a way of checking in on my clients. I always ask, "What about this current relationship is real? Are you running from someone or a situation or toward a real partnership?" An excellent way to know is if you are hoarding information about your relationship from others. If you are embarrassed or questioning your current state of affairs, speak up. Talk to your council, mentor, or coach. By keeping it real, you are being intentional about the love you want.

To run toward love, you have to be in a place to both give and receive love. We will talk a lot about what that specifically looks like in the upcoming chapters, but for now, here are a few prime examples of relationship-reality-check scenarios. See if you see yourself in any of these.

> Cyndee, a nurse, was looking for excitement in her life when she met Mike. He was a twice-divorced independently wealthy businessman. He had also been bankrupt multiple times but always beat the odds. His wealth afforded him houses all over the world. He lived to wine and dine pretty women, and all of his friends were along for the free ride. Cyndee spent the first year loading up her passport with trips beyond her imagination. She was in heaven until she realized the excursions were all there was. Mike was incapable of commitment. His money was the only thing he truly loved. Reality check: Cyndee spent the next few years looking for him to commit to the life she so desperately wanted. In the end, Mike was incapable of giving her

what she needed, although he had hit a home run in giving her what she wanted rescuing from.

Cam, a teacher in Colorado, was looking to settle down and get married. It was time. All of her friends were getting married, and her plan had always been to marry by the time she reached thirty. She was right on schedule, except Rodney was unaware of the plan. He was following his pursuits to become a football coach in the NFL when he met Cam at a party. A year into their courtship, he got a job offer on the West Coast. Her reality check came when Rodney did not ask her to move with him. Undeterred, Cam took fate into her own hands and made the trek to the West Coast anyway. To date, going on two years now, Cam has been waiting for his proposal. She has to ask herself: "Is Rodney what I want, or am I running toward a preset goal I had for my life?"

Stella, a public relations consultant, was in her late thirties when she met Joe, a trust fund baby, who was as handsome as a Ken doll but as immature as Pee-wee Herman. Stella had modeled throughout Europe before settling into the PR life. Her looks had always opened doors and garnered the attention she desired, but the offers had dwindled along with her youth. When Stella started dating Joe, everyone told them they looked just like Barbie and Ken. Stella felt she had met her equal and that babies would come next.

They got engaged within the first year but called it off multiple times while in the planning stages. Joe had turned out to be not just a looker but also a fighter. He was verbally abusive to Stella. She so desperately wanted Joe and his life to be her happily ever after that she sacrificed her self-respect for the sweeter things in life to get married.

At forty-four, she became pregnant after many years of fertility treatments. Her unfortunate reality check came while she was in labor. Joe was nowhere to be found and did not answer his cell phone, so her brother-in-law Doug went looking for him. Doug found Joe in bed with a neighbor. An argument ensued, and the cops were called. Joe drove to the hospital and started screaming throughout the labor and delivery ward. He was promptly arrested. Although Stella stayed for another year, they eventually divorced. His trust fund dried up, and Stella was left to fend for herself and her two children. Stella had been running from aging and what she viewed as a basic life toward the fantasy of what Joe represented.

In those three examples, we see women who were so busy running from something that they ran into an unintentional situation. Sure, they thought their intentions were on point, and they all desperately wanted to meet the right people. Nevertheless, they were not clear about their direction. Direction, not intention, determines our destination. Think about your intentions right now. Are they leading you to your final destination, or are you just making useless pit stops in the form of relationships?

We must get real clarity on what we want out of a relationship. If you say you want to have fun but deep down are looking for something deeper, you are not being intentional. Before you know it, if you don't get yourself in check, the fun guy may sneak up and become your husband. Let's play out the scenario. You are looking for fun, and meet a guy who likes to party. He has yet to find his passion in life, but you ignore that piece of the puzzle. Your initial intent is just to cut loose and have fun; however, you are not secure enough in your direction, so you follow his lead. Before you know it, you fall in love with the just-for-fun guy and end up married. A year in, you start to get clear about what you want. To build a life with, you want a mature man who has real ambition, but you settled. Do you see where your intention has to line up with your direction to get you to your desired destination? To establish intention, first you have to recognize that something that happened to you many, many years ago might be driving the ship.

ATTACHMENT STYLES

By now, you have probably accepted that much of how we both give and receive love comes from the model our parents have shown us. The British psychologist John Bowlby is best-known for his pioneering work around infants and how they form attachments early on, better known as the attachment theory. It is a psychological model that can describe the dynamics of long-term and short-term interpersonal relationships between humans. He studied how infants need to develop a connected relationship with a primary caregiver for their social and emotional development. Our style of attachment can affect our intention when picking a partner, and can affect how our relationships progress and also how they eventually end. Understanding how you form attachments and why can be an empowering building block to help you find the love you both want and need. The Psychology Today website has a free and quick Relationship Attachment Style Test you can take, but for now, I will give you a quick overview of four types of relationship styles.

> **Secure attachment:** If, as a child, you felt safe to venture out and explore the world, you most likely fall into this category. Because you were given the room and security to move around freely while still feeling loved, protected, and secure, you will do the same in your adult relationships. You feel free to ask for comfort when needed and can also give support when your partner is upset about something. A secure connection is mature, confident, honest, and respectful.
>
> People who fall into this category look for resolution in conflict. They are not afraid to be wrong and seek growth in communication. You want one of your relationship council members, probably the mentor, to have this type of connection to his or her partner. In this relationship, both parties are free to grow and seek while maintaining their bond.
>
> **Anxious-Ambivalent attachment:** Just the type name alone may cause anxiety. The reason is that people in this category are eager to bond. They need rescuing and will require a relationship reality check. Instead of love toward a partner, they feel an almost engulfing hunger.

They are looking for an outside person not only to validate their existence but to complete them. They come across as needy and clingy but often tend to push their partners away to see if they will come back. They seek control because they feel so out of control in their everyday lives.

I have seen many healthy people get connected to someone in the Anxious-Ambivalent attachment category only to walk away out of complete exhaustion. The constant need for validation can kill any spark. When a healthy person starts to look for independence, many times the anxious person will begin to feel unsafe and try to take situational control. He or she interprets a partner's freedom as an affirmation that the partner will indeed leave. These people are often suspicious, take things too personally, and constantly worry that they have offended someone.

Jennifer's attachment style was Anxious-Ambivalent, while her boyfriend's was Secure. In the beginning, they spent every waking second together. They had pet names for each other and could never keep their hands off each other. As the attraction phase eventually led to the commitment phase, Jennifer's constant need for validation started to exhaust Scott. He loved her and was in love with her. He had committed to their relationship and felt excited about their future. But the more time he started to spend exploring other activities and hobbies, the more anxious Jennifer got. She would call or text him always looking for reassurance. At first Scott obliged, but as the months turned into years, he started to tire of feeling he was solely responsible for her emotional well-being.

Jennifer's parents had divorced when she was an infant. Her mother, an alcoholic, had been in and out of treatment. As a child, Jennifer had been left alone a lot, leaving her longing for security. In Scott she found the holy grail. Scott understood her past and tried his best to help her feel loved and cherished. But he also began to tell little white lies to get the freedom he needed. He would add an hour or two to his appointments to get time at the gym or more time playing golf with his buddies, until Jennifer put a tracker on his phone and found out.

"She had a complete meltdown," Scott said when telling me about their fight. "She got so mad that when she turned around to stomp off, she fell right over my golf clubs! We both started to laugh. Thank God. My lying stopped right then and there. I did not want to see her so hurt. I just wanted to make everything okay." It is not up to our partners to carry the load we are unwilling to unpack. Jennifer and Scott have since found ways to form a Secure-type attachment in their relationship. Scott is upfront and honest, and Jennifer, through trial-and-error, has started to trust their bond.

> **Dismissive-Avoidant attachment:** Many times, people who have experienced abandonment identify with this style of attachment. These people have learned to occupy themselves, and in relationships will emotionally distance themselves from their loved one. They can shut down entirely if needed and seemingly emotionally detach during an argument. They can be loners and isolate themselves when deep down all they want is a connection.
>
> **Fearful-Avoidant attachment:** This attachment style swings on a pendulum between being too

close to someone and feeling distant. People in this category attempt to keep their emotions intact but play mental gymnastics trying to. They are pulled toward chaos and live between the highs and lows of a relationship. For them, the timing always seems to be off in love. Fearful-Avoidant attachment types look for any way they can to avoid and distance themselves from others. In relationships, they will become workaholics or may even find themselves using addictive behaviors to self-soothe. They yearn for a loving connection but cannot throw caution to the wind and go for it. When faced with real commitment, they become increasingly uncomfortable with intimacy and run away before anything becomes too serious.

Andy had a Fearful-Avoidant attachment style. Deep down, he wanted to commit but couldn't. He dated Nikki for eight years and still had not committed. She was ready for the next chapter and wanted to make babies and live in the suburbs. Instead, he busied himself with work and climbing the corporate ladder. He had worked every single holiday and missed countless weddings, graduations, and other events with family and friends.

When Nikki finally grew tired of his ever-growing disconnection, she tried everything to get his attention and turn their ship around. The more she came toward him, the more he distanced himself. He took up residence on their sofa and fell asleep every night with his computer on his lap. Nikki finally left him.

She had spent a total of ten years trying to get him to commit to loving her. He made weak attempts to get her back, but the truth was, he wanted to be alone. Looking back, Nikki realized she had known something was amiss from the beginning, when she noticed that Andy's parents seemed disconnected, too. His mother was the Fearful-Avoidant type and followed his father's lead. She never used her voice, and Nikki had initially thought of the father as misogynistic.

But she had ignored the initial warning signs that Andy was not capable of any long-term commitment. She could not fully understand the insecure attachments Andy had formed in early childhood. He was taught to avoid feelings at all costs. Nikki was taught to feel free. Andy was cognitively handicapped in that he could never quite get out of his head long enough to get into his real life. It's not to say that they could not have worked this out. They most certainly could have, but Andy was paralyzed with fear and found it just too unsafe to take that leap.

C H A P T E R   7

HOW RELATIONSHIPS WORK—AND HOW TO DO RELATIONSHIPS BETTER

Have you heard the song "Happier" by Marshmello? I listened to my daughter singing the lyrics the other day, and it hit me how relevant they are to this chapter. We have talked a lot about your past relationships, and how your family of origin plays a part in who you pick, how you get triggered, and how you deal with conflict. At this point in the process, you may need to raise your caution flag. Here is a question to ponder: Are you causing your problems by going back to your triggers and learned inner conflict? If the answer is "maybe," do not fret. There is still so much to learn about relationships. In this chapter, we are going to break down how relationships work. When do you stay and when do you leave?

The song "Happier" is about a relationship that has reached its tail end, yet still, somehow, the singer wants to hold on; however, deep down within him, he knows that the only way his significant other can be happier is by abandoning the relationship and by their both going their separate ways. Does that sound familiar? At some point in our lives, we all reach this crossroads in a relationship or two, or three. Maybe the person we are in a relationship with is a total narcissist or simply ill-fitted. Whatever the case, we are torn about whether we should stay or go.

Leaving is not easy. Leaving someone you still love but who is not right for you can be excruciating. So, I started thinking, "How do I convince you that what is on the other side of your being happy is, in fact, intention?" I have witnessed so many men and women get to the edge of change and stop. Why do they stop? Two ugly sisters: fear and worry. Fear of never finding anyone else, and worry that they will end up alone mired in regret. Then then become paralyzed and refuse to budge. Well, that is no fun!

An easy way to get the sisters out of your way is to set your intention to not let worry and fear run your life. First, ask yourself if the concern you are feeling is even valid. Do you think you will never find someone to love you? The likelihood of that is almost zero if you have a strong intention to be loved. To change your narrative and put those sisters in a much-needed timeout, reframe your intentions. It may sound something like this: "The chance of meeting and falling in love again is just as strong for me as it is for anyone else. I intend to meet someone divinely suited for me. I am lovable. I deserve love, and it will come to me quickly."

Once you have your new intention verbiage, take it a step further by visualizing that love. What does it look like? How does it feel? Allow yourself to feel unconditional, steadfast love for longer than you hung out with the sisters. Give the sisters a solid ten minutes. Then give your new narrative twenty minutes to have center stage. Every time your mind starts to go back to the ugly sisters, redirect it. By staying with your new narrative, you are teaching your brain to redirect from a negative to a positive. It feels good. The more you practice changing your narrative through intentional practices, the better you will feel. But don't just trust me. Science has also proven my process.

Not too long ago, I watched a fantastic documentary on Netflix entitled *Happy*, about, well, happiness. In it, Sonja Lyubomirsky, a professor at the University of California, Riverside, and author of *The How of Happiness: A New Approach to Getting the Life You Want*, breaks down what determines happiness. She found through her studies that our genetics preset 50 percent of our happiness (I know, I know), 40 percent of our happiness comes from intentional activities, and only 10 percent is derived from life circumstances. I know; I was shocked, too.

Per science, we can't change our genetics. They are preset and resistant to our changing them or trying to control them. We can, however, try to change our circumstances, but how long does that work? I am sure some of you have learned the hard way by attempting to change your life circumstances to be happier. The thing is, moving away, changing jobs, or even changing our outward appearance may boost our mood in the short term, but in the end, we are still left with what is between our ears. To be intentional and get to that sweet 40 percent, we can't sit around and try to be content. We have to move, evolve, and change the narrative of how we view our lives.

Believe it or not, by pursuing my process, you are putting that sweet spot to the test. You are making things happen by challenging yourself to find new ways of thinking and seeking better ways to experience a more significant, more profound love not just for yourself but for your future partner. You are learning to take your power back by asserting some control over your thoughts and feelings. In summary, all that you intend to do will have a long-lasting effect on your overall happiness. You just have to leave the ugly sisters in the closet.

I WILL SURVIVE!

There is no mistaking that my favorite go-to karaoke song is "I Will Survive" by Gloria Gaynor. I am playing it in the background and singing the lyrics as I type this. Not to sound corny, but it is a damn good comeback song no matter how old you are. Gloria reminds us that we can survive any breakup, hiccup, or disaster that threatens to take us out. We discussed in a previous chapter the difference between weak love and strong love. Let's now take a look at where you might be at this very moment in life.

Is it time to walk away from a weak love? Are you getting mixed signals? If so, go ahead and take that as a "no go"—meaning, anyone who has you questioning your status with him or her is confused. A confused person cannot give you a straight answer, no matter how many times you ask. No amount of dramatic walk-outs, hang-ups, or ultimatums is going to fix the problem until the person who is confused can get the clarity he or she needs, and that may take months or even years. Who has the time or the ego to wait for someone else to decide the future? Not you. You are too sexy and busy to let anyone control your destiny.

Jenny, a thirty-two-year-old broker, had been getting mixed signals from Tommy for four years. When he met Jenny, he had told her point-blank that he was not looking for anything long-term, yet a few months in he was saying "I love you" and giving Jenny every reason to think his narrative was shifting into a more long-term outlook.

But another year passed with Tommy refusing to talk real commitment. He was giving mixed signals by saying he did not want a commitment while continuing to play house with

Jenny. He was getting his cake and eating it, too. Jenny finally decided to break up with him but continued to talk to him via email and text.

In the middle of Jenny's efforts to get him to relaunch, someone notified her that Tommy had gone on a dinner date with his ex-girlfriend. Jenny, who was furious, drove straight to his house and confronted him. He then did the whole bait-and-switch thing, telling Jenny that she had broken up with him, and therefore it was her fault that they were in this mess! Jenny was beside herself and got back with him out of fear of being left alone after speaking up for herself. This cycle repeated itself for the next year, with him saying he and his ex were merely friends with a history and that Jenny was his one true love.

Tommy was an emotional vampire—a toxic person who takes over another person's thoughts and drains him or her, leaving the other person feeling emotionally exhausted. Emotional vampires suck the life out of their victims by provoking emotional reactions in them so they can feed off their emotions and resources. There are a few ways to spot one of these little suckers, and Jenny felt all of them. Here are the characteristics of emotional vampires:

- They make everything about them regularly by starting any conversation with words like "I" or "me."
- Their favorite role to play is the victim.
- They talk in circles and leave you drained.
- They cause you constant frustration because you feel so misunderstood.
- They are controlling regarding not only your thoughts but your time, too.

Ladies, don't get sucked in. In Jenny's case, she is getting stuck in a Bermuda Triangle. Tommy, like all emotional vampires, will continue to wear her completely down for as long as she allows it. In short, if a partner is not headed in the same direction as you are, it is best to change your direction early. Assure yourself that you are worth it. Check your intentions and keep going. There is nothing emotional vampires can do when you don't let them have a feeding frenzy. Remember, you are the one in control of how you want to be loved. If the person you are in a relationship with is bringing you constant heartbreak, frustration, and worry, that person is not "the one." Period.

SURVIVING A BREAKUP—AND THRIVING!

Let's say you are in a situation like Jenny's or in a relationship that has run its course, and you know you have to end it. Everyone on your relationship council is onboard with your breaking it off, and in your heart, you know they are right. There is an actual way to have a healthy, drama-free breakup and even thrive afterward. Here are three stages of the breakup process, for when you are ready:

1. **Acceptance.** You have probably spent a considerable amount of emotional and physical energy loving this person. You will need to consolidate the positive memories and compare them with the reasons you have gotten to this place. Accept that it is natural to have love for the person you spent so much time with and also be ready to let that person go.

2. **Acknowledgment.** It is okay to acknowledge the good. Acknowledge in your mind and with others the reason you were drawn to the person and your shared experi-

ences. This part of the process will continue even after you have done the deed. Let it.

3. **Anxiety.** Knowing that the end is near can bring on a considerable amount of stress. You may question yourself by going back and forth about whether you should break up or not. It is necessary to grieve the end of the relationship, and you may even start doing so while you are still in it. Breaking up is just that. Two people go off on their separate ways. By uncoupling, both people will now be expected to begin to deal with their emotions on their own and with the help of their support systems. It is no longer something the two of you will need to do together.

I am not saying that breakups are a clean line. What I am saying is that being truthful about what you want moving forward is of the utmost importance. Confusion will lead only to pain for everyone. The finality of it all can be brutal in many ways. Each person has to find ways to cope and start getting on with a new life couple-free. It can take a heap of emotional intelligence to be both sympathetic and empathetic. Putting yourself in the other person's shoes will allow you to see the breakup from his or her vantage point. Use that empathy to consider how your actions or reactions may be harmful to the person's moving on. Try to respect the new direction and get on with moving on toward loving strong.

THE BREAKUP PROCESS

1. **Do it in person.** Don't avoid feeling the emotions by doing it over text or email. By meeting in person, you can both can feel free to emote and say your peace.

2. **Be honest.** I cannot tell you how incredibly important it is to say the truth. I have seen so many clients get stuck in the abyss just waiting for answers or trying their best to understand the other person's reasoning because the person who broke up with them was not honest. This is unfair and weak.

3. **Break up as many times as it takes.** I know this one sounds counterproductive, but sometimes it takes a few times to make it stick. Humans are not perfect. Sometimes we need a few test runs. Just be honest along the way. Do not stay in something or go back if you know in your heart you want out. Be clear. Give the other person specifics as to why you want to end it. Respect always follows honesty.

4. **Give the other person a platform.** Let the person vent and emote. Listen and, when you can, clear up any misconceptions. Don't give false hope. Giving false hope reduces the other person's ability to move on effectively.

5. **Don't air dirty laundry.** Inevitably both people lose initially in a breakup. Don't take to social media to become passive-aggressive. You can always tell when a person starts posting quotes that they are dealing with some unresolved emotions. Do it in private with friends, family, a coach, or even a therapist.

6. **Don't rally the troops.** Do not waste your time trying to get mutual friends to pick a side to deal with any tangled emotions. Be upfront with your needs and remain empathetic to your ex's. It may behoove you to take a breather from social media for a while during your grieving process. Anger is just not cute.

7. **Take time.** Give yourself time to mourn the relationship. Do things that bring you joy, and also allow yourself to

feel pain. If you don't, you will end up with another weak love. Write in a journal, take walks, or do whatever else feels useful to you in those moments of deep sadness. I promise you will survive.

8. **Set up a check-in time.** Sometimes I tell my clients to set up a check-in time after the breakup has happened to clear up any questions or lingering emotions. It can be done via the phone or even in person. It may also be to exchange personal items or give one last goodbye hug. If this check-in time is being used as a way to get the person back, you may need to go back to the first chapter and read the difference between loving weak and loving strong to figure out which way to go.

9. **Be proud.** Pat yourself on the back for walking away from a person or situation that did not offer you strong love. Know your truth and stick to it. Live intentionally.

10. **Ask for support.** Tell friends and family what you need and don't need. Stick with the advice from your relationship council. Trust that they have your back and trust in your decisions. You will be rewarded.

THE PHASES OF A RELATIONSHIP

You may not be in the breakup stage at all. You may even be in the early stages of new love. You are starting to understand that intention leads to direction and direction leads to the destination; however, you still are not entirely sure if the new guy or gal you are crushing on is right. Many women don't know the normal progression of a relationship because they may have never seen it firsthand or experienced it in their own home growing up.

Again, you are most likely here for one of two reasons. Either you have stumbled and fallen hard with "the guy," or you have completely put yourself on sabbatical, refusing to invest in finding love. If you are here because of "the guy," it is time to pull up your big-girl panties and change your narrative from feeling broken to appreciating the beautiful mirror that the relationship has provided you. Because of the pain, the universe is giving you the time to reflect—the time needed to value your worth and who you are, and the space to validate what you want. If you are here because you have kept yourself protected by disallowing yourself love, do a celebratory dance. You are ready to find strong love.

To get back to basics, let's look at the phases of a relationship. Read through them below and think about where you have been or where you are heading now. Can you identify which phase you usually get stumped in?

> **The Attraction phase:** This is the fun part. The Attraction phase is also called the "honeymoon phase," because everything seems perfect at this stage. You feel healthy during the first phase of the relationship. You feel lust, physical attraction, and intrigue. It may be instant or gradual, but either way, you are excited. All you can think about is the other person. You may find yourself perusing his social media accounts or wondering what he is doing during the day, because your mind is consumed with the possibility of finding love. Dopamine, the "cool neurotransmitter," rushes through your body every time you see or hear from him. You are on cloud nine and believe that anything is possible…because it is. "I can give and receive love easily," is your motto. You are in a constant state of bliss.

You can always tell when someone is in this alluring phase, because everything he or she says or thinks goes back to the newfound crush—everything. Like, if you are with a girl-friend who is in this phase with a new fellow and are talking about going to the beach for a girl's weekend, your friend who is crushing hard may say something like, "I would love to go to the beach. Zack likes the beach, too. Did you know his family vacations every year in Destin, Florida? Isn't that awesome? I always wanted to meet someone who loves the beach as much as I do." In the Attraction phase, we find a way to bring everything back to our intense attraction. It is all we can think about, which is why it is so intoxicating.

Green flag: It is easy to keep going during this phase, as it may be based on physical attraction alone. If he is pursuing you and making you feel cherished and respected during this phase, keep going. This connection may have a chance to go somewhere lovely.

Red flag: Does he have a bad reputation, or has he already flopped when you had plans? Pay close attention here. How are you feeling? This phase should be the easiest. If he starts out shady, it may be your cue to walk.

Stumped? You may feel stumped because you are not instantly attracted to him. Yes, attraction is a big part of a relationship. But don't write him off because he has freckles or drives a

Honda. Give it some time. The three-date rule can be a great litmus test for attraction. If after three dates and a kiss, there are no sparks, it may be time to walk away and throw him into the friend category.

The Courting phase: Butterflies and rainbows are still showing up in this phase; however, uncertainty is settling in on some levels. The cool neurotransmitter, dopamine, is always accompanying you on your dates, and now it has even brought its friend adrenaline along. The excitement is palpable. A kiss may also have you seeing fireworks. You are beginning to home in on your deepest desires and hopes that something long-term may be in the future. You want to learn everything there is to know about him, and you two have long talks about your beliefs, dreams, and desires. You are both adjusting to the reality of the new relationship. You are beginning to see who he is. Believe him when he shows you.

Green flag: The desires you both have for a future relationship are lining up. He is on his best behavior, and when there is any hint of conflict, he is open to working it out together. Your relationship council should also be digging him at this point.

Red flag: He has stopped courting you or putting your needs first. You are starting to see that all the things are not lining up. Minor to significant conflicts are arising and are triggering old wounds or patterns. Ask yourself, "Is he bringing out the best in me or causing me to feel insecure or sad?" Don't pull a Lola and try to make a fling into your forever dude.

Stumped? Ask yourself, "How is the courting going? Is he giving me the attention I desire? Am I expecting too much?" If you have a lot of male energy because of the lack of a male figure in your life, make sure you don't try to take over here. Let yourself be courted. If you are feeling unsettled or uncertain about something in this phase, take inventory. Where are these feelings coming from? Are they fear-driven? What keeps coming up that you may still need to do some work around?

If you are a fan of NBC's *The Bachelor* or *The Bachelorette*, you have gotten a crash course on how relationships work and don't work and how they can be done better. As a dating person, you can uphold only your part of the partnership. You have zero control over what another person does or says, but you do have every bit of power over how you choose to react to someone else's actions. Take Hannah B., the bachelorette on season fifteen. Hannah had a few disastrous relationships unfold in front of our very eyes on the television screen. The first was with a guy named Luke P., who seemed to every one of the men in the house to be a master manipulator, but to Hannah, he appeared to be her knight in shining armor. Her first impression of him blew her away, and immediately she made him a front-runner in her mind. It took many episodes with everyone around her telling her that he was not who he seemed for her to take off her blinders and figure it out.

The moment of reckoning came when he, in her words, "slut-shamed" her for having sex in one of the fantasy suites. After Luke P. was kicked off, she had to decide between three other seemingly stand-up men. Two of them would turn out to be who they said they were by continuing to prove their character through each week of emotional upheaval and adversity.

Still, Hannah ended up choosing a guy named Jed, a country singer from Nashville, at the final rose ceremony. Soon after they got engaged on national TV, a story broke that Jed had a girlfriend back home, whom he had left to be on *The Bachelorette* to gain exposure for his singing career and not to find love. When *People* magazine broke the story, Hannah was shocked and called off the engagement on live TV to the gasps and applause of the in-studio crowd.

I tell you this story not just because I get pulled into the show season after season, but because it's a true, albeit fast-for-warded version, of what we can go through in our dating lives while trying to find a love that is strong and true.

In the end, Hannah B. knew for sure what type of man she wanted to marry. Jed's apparent shortcomings and lack of ability to be upfront and honest throughout the process proved to be his downfall. Hannah was forced to do her breaking up for the world to see. She even told the host, Chris Harrison, that there was a time in her life that she would have stayed in a relationship like that and tried to make it work, but because she now knew her worth, she was not willing to sacrifice her love-strong goals by settling for a guy whose track record was a little suspect.

The Idealization phase: Our brains have the uncanny ability to idealize someone when feelings of lust or love set in. In this phase, uncertainty is usual. It is where you weigh the pros and cons of life with the other person. In this phase, you still believe anything is possible and challenges can easily be overcome. This phase is also when your friends and family pose questions to keep you grounded. Pay attention and give yourself time to reflect on what is going on within you and with the other person.

Green flag: He is even better than you could have ever imagined. Your time together keeps getting better and better. You feel happy and open to a long-term relationship. You both bring out the best in each other, and friends and family on both sides take notice.

Red flag: Are you falling for him or the idea of him? Do you genuinely want the same things? Are you stuck in the fantasy of it all, or are you falling for a guy who best suits your needs? If in your gut you know it is not right, listen. If he is upsetting you or causing you more hurt than happiness, you may be in for a lifetime of pain. What lesson keeps coming up for you?

Stumped? Although you may see some small red flags, you may choose to ignore them. This is where you may have decided to put things on mute in the past. Pay attention. I know it is all roses and champagne here, but can this guy be a good partner for you? Staying focused on your deal-breakers is essential. It is vital to see the other person for who he is. Listen and continue

to appraise the situation. Don't be afraid to ask
your partner questions during this time.

Lola is one of the most fun women I have ever coached. She was making her living as a salsa instructor, and met whom she thought was the man of her dreams while on tour dancing. Lola was in love with love. She was enamored with the first phase of a relationship (when the man is in pursuit) and felt powerful, almost invincible. When she met Carl, it was as if time stopped for her. He was a powerful dancer and drew him to her like a magnet. She said that while watching him dance for the first time, she felt herself almost levitate.

They began a torrid affair, but Carl was a ladies' man, much like Lola's father, and soon she was in his grips. In a few short months, the newness had worn off. Carl had begun to lose interest. Gone were those intense lovemaking sessions after a great show; now Carl would rather smoke cigars with his boys and flirt with the cocktail waitresses. Lola was beside herself with worry when I met her. She did not understand what had happened, and her primary goal was to get him back and to have him focus on her 100 percent.

Many women get stuck in the Idealization phase with a partner. They are in such lust that they forget their boundaries when questions or concerns arise early in the relationship. Because Carl and Lola were in the first six months of their relationship, she did not want to come off as too pushy, so she kept her mouth shut when he displayed behaviors that she never would have put up with before. The allure of a ladies' man can be like lightning in a bottle for some women. They want to catch it because they, too, feel lit up when they are in the guy's laser focus. It can be intoxicating.

However, as my grandfather used to warn me: If a man comes on too strong and too fast, he will leave just as quickly.

Lola's dad was a jazz singer. He traveled and had a legion of fans who followed him across the country. Lola was mesmerized by her father and loved how electric the house felt when he was home. When she met Carl, it was as if she had a part of her father back. She and Carl had a roller coaster relationship full of the highest highs and the lowest lows. What Lola came to realize is this: Carl should have been just a fling, but instead, he was her mirror. Her subconscious translation was: Real love is always exciting. You have to throw caution to the wind because it may last for only a moment in time before it is gone.

Lola and I did a lot of work around her father-daughter relationship. She missed her father so much, and sadly he passed away before he could get off the road and be a full-time dad. We worked on her understanding of the phases in a long-term relationship. She had to learn to embrace them all to get what she ultimately wanted: marriage and children.

> **The Love phase:** Although the excitement and euphoria start to die down at this point in your relationship, don't be alarmed. All of the feel-good hormones and neurotransmitters are slowly being replaced by even more significant rewards, such as trust and a deepening attachment to your partner. You are beginning to feel the calmness of your unity. Stability is what is on the menu in this phase. You should be feeling positive about where your relationship is headed. Plans for the future are a reasonable topic of discussion, and friends and family are a regular part of the mix. A long-term commitment, such as marriage,

may be on the table. The Love phase comes in strong at about eighteen months to two years into the relationship.

Green flag: You continue to fall deeper and deeper in love with this person. You have finally found a person you want to grow with, and he or she wants to build a life with you. You find ease in being together, and you are being your true, authentic self. Both of your histories are accepted, and you have worked through almost all of your differences. There is a natural flow to your union.

Red flag: Feelings of boredom are common here, but true commitment should be established. Any transgressions or cheating should raise a flag here. Any breakdown of trust can be a deal-breaker in this phase. If there is verbal, physical, or emotional abuse, you have to walk away.

Stumped? You could be scared, and some of your old issues may be trying to show up here. Be open about where you are, and seek any additional guidance you may need to help you along the way. Contentment should be the overarching theme at this point in your union. You believe you have found the perfect partner for yourself, and are ready and willing to do any work it may take to keep this relationship front and center in your life.

If you are stumped, be sure to recognize that wondering if you could start over with someone else is normal. You may be missing the early

stages of lust and excitement. Make sure you
weigh the pros and cons before doing anything
crazy in a moment of weakness.

EXERCISE: IDENTIFY PAST RELATIONSHIPS' PHASES

I hope that by learning the phases of a relationship, you can
see the areas you tend to get stumped by. Many women I have
coached seem to get stuck in the same areas in relationships. For
this exercise, I want you to write down each of your past relationships beside each phase. See where they may have gone off
track or where you may have put blinders on. Are you all over the
board, or do you get stuck in one phase?

BOUNDARIES

It's vital to learn about boundaries. Most relationship missteps
are a result of flimsy boundaries. For our purposes, we will define
"boundary" as a line that shows where one person begins and
the other ends. This will stand as your universal rule about what
is acceptable behavior and what is not. With boundaries, it is
essential to feel right about the standards you require for someone to be an intimate part of your life. You must be clear with
your partner about who you are, what you are willing to accept,
and what your deal-breakers are. Healthy boundaries allow you
to have self-respect and share personal information when you are
ready, and also empower you to make healthy choices without the
responsibility of someone else's feelings.

Unhealthy boundaries let us feel responsible for someone
else's feelings, share too much too soon, or allow others to make
our decisions for us. If you find yourself giving in to others at

your own expense out of guilt or obligation, and you're unable to express and act on your true feelings, you probably have faulty boundaries. There is no fun in that game. If you have a track record of this, it may be time to pump the brakes and put up some healthy boundaries.

We attract people and partners by putting out into the universe what we feel we need or deserve at that time. We will continue to attract the ones who need to teach us lessons until we stop choosing fear and instead choose to love strong. If you are sick and tired of the roadblocks or playing the victim, it may be time to have some real big-girl boundaries to prevent you from falling back down the same damaged holes. A lack of strong boundaries takes us out of the driver's seat and puts us right into the victim's chair. When we lack strong boundaries, we build resentment.

To ensure that you always working from a place of love and not fear, you have to a) choose how you want to see any given situation, and b) choose how you want to react to it. By acting out of a place of self-love, you will bring about a positive shift and transform old patterns into radically new ways to have relationships. Think back to your past relationships. Did you have healthy boundaries? Did he? Looking back, if boundaries were set, would the two of you have been happier or gone up in smoke? Would boundaries have stopped you from wasting time on someone who was not right for you?

We adopt many of our fears in childhood. The universal concerns are being rejected or abandoned, and feeling unworthy of love. Those fears cause our egos to take charge. The first step in understanding your boundaries—or lack of them—is awareness. By identifying which fear is causing you to react in a way that does not honor your self-love, you can start to shift your reactions to it.

Some fear-based reactions are:

- Not wanting to upset the other person for fear of his or her leaving
- Valuing the other person's opinions more than your own for fear of being rejected
- Not standing in your power because you have never been given the space to know your worth

The next step is to choose love over fear. Most of what we never fear happens. By based on what we discussed earlier, ask yourself what about the fear is real. By changing the narrative around the fear, you will be choosing self-love. It takes practice to continue to choose love over fear. It is an ongoing intentional act, and by changing the narrative each time concern arises, you will change your life.

The final step is to use your voice. By connecting to your boundaries and acting on them, you will be honoring your voice. The more you speak up, the more comfortable you will be regarding what you deserve in relationships. The more you voice your thoughts and opinions, the more you will be in healthy types of relationships where respect is mutual.

EXERCISE: IDENTIFY YOUR BOUNDARIES

For this exercise, write down your boundaries. If you are uncertain how to use your voice, go back to each relationship and write down what you know you deserved at the major crossroads in it. What should you have said? What boundaries should you have set? Which fear kept you from setting them?

Boundaries can be tricky for anyone who is not used to using them. It is a process that may change and grow as you do. Your behavior has to be in line with the boundaries you set, so take your time. Be true to yourself. Practice self-care and don't over-complicate things. If you find yourself overanalyzing, apologizing, or going back on your newly identified boundaries, stop and do a gut check. You picked up this book because you wanted to know why you got stuck on the guy. Don't be afraid to have those on your relationship council fact-check to see if they agree with your flags and boundaries. We've all got you.

PART III:
FOUNDATION FOR THE FUTURE

CHAPTER 8

THE MESSAGE IN THE MIRROR: LOOKING AT YOURSELF TO SOLVE RELATIONSHIP PROBLEMS

I am a resource hog. For years I have been obsessed with finding out every single thing I can about love. I read books on love. I study and analyze the process of love and heartbreak ad nauseam. It all started when I found my mother's encyclopedia-size book on horoscope matching beside her nightstand in high school. I had seen her pull it out on many occasions, whether she was helping a friend with her love life or using it to understand her own. To me, that book held many of the secrets to finding a match. I went on to use it to help my friends and me find the love we wanted in our formative years. Upon having a new crush, I would rush home to see whether our birthdates meant compatibility magic. If the forecast was that we would not be a good match, I took it to heart. If the book of horoscopes predicted a good match, I would give it a go.

There is just something about the power of love and what it provides for us that feeds my insatiable hunger to always want to know more. With love, I am not picky or judgmental in my quest to find the answers, either. I routinely take both conventional and unconventional routes to learn more and more. I have consulted and learned from psychic mediums, shamans, coaches, preachers, books, therapists, gurus, experts, married couples, dating couples, singles…the list goes on and on. It is through all of this analysis and study over the decades that I have come to rely on a few expert tools to help people better understand themselves, what makes them tick, and why they feel the way they do.

Before homing in on the specific tools I use today for my methodology, I did what many women do and looked outward for answers. I even consulted a palm reader, and yes, there was a fluorescent pink blinking light in her window in the shape of a palm. I was stuck on "the guy" and spent more money and effort than I would like to admit trying to understand him. I just wanted someone, anyone, to tell me that all was going to be okay. At that point in my life, depending on myself to pull me out of my funk was not even on my radar. I was in Chicago visiting a girlfriend, Amy, when we decided to go to a comedy show to get me out of my head. As we were crossing the road to get in line to see the show, I could see the pink fluorescent light calling my name. I told Amy I wanted to see the psychic. Ever the trooper, she was down to go with me after the show was over. In a panic, because all I could think about was "the guy," I ran down the street to see if the palm reader could work me in before the show. I got to the front door and knocked. After a few impatient minutes, I rang the old doorbell but heard no sound coming from the other side of the door. Then I noticed a small sign that said "come on in" hanging above the door.

As I opened the door, a bell jingled overhead. I shut the door and looked up the steps to see a mysterious woman coming toward me wearing a bohemian-looking mumu that fell down each step after her like a wedding veil. "Hi," I said nervously. "Can I by any chance get a quick reading before my comedy show starts in twenty minutes?" She smiled warmly and asked me to follow her up the stairs to her office. Behind a waterfall of colorful hanging crystal beads, she took her seat on a make-shift sofa tucked away in what must have once been a laundry room. She asked me to have a seat on the opposite side of her on a mound of red and purple satin pillows. She began feverishly flipping over cards and nodding while rocking back and forth on her makeshift sofa, which looked to be made of cushions cov-ered with a satin sheet. She reminded me of a mix of Whoopi Goldberg and Erykah Badu.

The candle in front of me on the small table was the only light. I thought about my mother. What would Amy tell her if someone grabbed me while I was in this house? I was so desperate for answers, I didn't even care. The palm reader, Millie, went on to tell me that my guy was not "the one." She said I would marry in my late thirties, have two children, and need back surgery.

Devastated, I got up and tried to thank her before the tears started to fall as I did the walk of shame back down the old car-peted stairs. I realized just how low I had gotten. I had left Amy, whom I had not seen in over a year, to save our spot in line while I confided in a palm reader. When I wasn't glued to my TV set crying over Hallmark movies, I was eating pizza and crying while slurping down a milkshake. I was spending all of my time trying to figure him out instead of working to understand myself. It was not my best moment. Although I think in many ways I lost a good two years of my twenties, the experience shaped the person I would become. From that heartbreak, I went on a boundless quest to encourage women to understand themselves better to get the strong love they want. It was through that awareness and time in my life that my methodology began to take shape. If it were not for my heartbreak, I would not be writing this book today. As a side note, the palm reader was right. I got married again at thirty-nine, had neck surgery the day after I got engaged, and had two amazing children in succession.

THE ENNEAGRAM

We are the means of our experiences, and each experience teaches us a lesson. We learn what to take with us and what to leave behind. As we have discussed throughout this book, the one thing we can't leave behind is ourselves. The more we learn about ourselves, the better equipped we are to understand our actions and reactions toward others. One of my go-to tools to help with this understanding is the Enneagram. I came upon the Enneagram while learning about how to become a better communicator in corporate America. When coaching women or speaking, I routinely incorporate its lessons. The word "enneagram" stems from the Greek words "*ennea*" (nine) and *grammos* (a written symbol); it is a system that covers nine personality types in terms of relating to the self, others, and the world around us. It is a tool that has been written about and studied over and over around the world because of its ability to help people understand their personality types. For our purposes, the Enneagram should serve as a guide for better understanding how to deal with conflict and solve relationship communication issues.

The Enneagram combines traditional real-world wisdom with psychology. It can serve as a unique and powerful tool for understanding ourselves and the people we choose to love by showing us the strengths and weaknesses of each personality type. Each person's personality type is derived from childhood. Yes, it goes right back to dear old Mom and Dad again. We are all motivated by core messaging that we received consciously or subconsciously in childhood. We all have core issues in the forms of fear, want, weakness, and things we crave. Our core fears are based on what we spend our lives avoiding, such as abandonment or inadequacy. Our core want is what we are always striving for that we believe will bring us the ultimate happiness, such as being loved without conditions. Another core is based on a weakness we are always wrestling with, such as envy, resentment, or greed. Then there is the core we crave, which is connecting to our heart's desire, such as being taken care of, wanted, and accepted.

To better understand your childhood messaging, which is connected to your core issues and desires, pick a statement from the nine listed below that speaks to or resonates with you.

1. I should not make mistakes. There is a right way and a wrong way to do things.
2. I should not have needs of my own. I should help others first.
3. I should not have my own emotions or feelings.
4. I am too much or not enough for most people.
5. I should not put my trust in others.
6. I should not trust myself to do the right thing.
7. I cannot depend on others for anything in this world.
8. I should not trust others or allow myself to depend on others.
9. I should not be too loud or assert myself. I am not that important.

One of these statements should speak to your inner child. The statement, or something close to it, is what has shaped who you are today and how you present yourself out in the world. It is important to note that many of us have a few different numbers. While one number may be your dominant personality type, you may also relate to a few others. Below I will summarize each type. Look for the descriptors of each personality type to determine your number.

Type 1: The Reformer or Perfectionist. Although they are calm, type ones can be uncompromising and even judgmental at times. They are quiet scorekeepers who insist on there being a right way and a wrong way of doing things. They tend to keep their feelings and emotions quiet and have high emotional maturity; however, type ones can lead a life of dissatisfaction because they always want to fix everything around them, and their lack of control leaves them feeling as though their job is never done. They may have to-do lists a mile long and are not able to relax until every single thing is off the list. They can be hard on themselves, because their inner critic likes to scold them for not doing things perfectly.

In relationships, type ones may make their partners feel judged. This all comes from not feeling good enough themselves. They long to get it right. In conflict, it is crucial for type ones to be able to express themselves without fear of judgment, or they will feel resentment toward their partners. If they are not being heard, they can become judgmental and give off more of a teacher vibe by correcting versus compromising. If you are the partner of a type one, it is your job to encourage your partner, for he or she craves getting it right. When type ones are loved, they are sincere and reasonable, and make every person around them feel cared for. The best way to communicate with a type one is to ask how you can help. Be supportive during problem-solving. Be gentle and affirming. Offer appreciation.

Joe, age thirty-six, is a type one, according to Dana. Dana says, "I know when Joe is building resentment in his mind against me because he gets quiet and even holds his breath when I challenge him. I have learned that when I criticize him, he shuts down. I am a type seven, so being direct is just part of my makeup. I have asked him to give me more clarity about how he is feeling, and I, in turn, give more grace and compassion when we are in conflict."

Type 2: The Advisor. Advisors are helpful and supportive; they thrive on acts of service and being needed. They have a natural ability to love and care for others, leaving not much time for themselves. Many type twos are inherently intuitive and can feel others' pain. People flock to them for their nurturing ways, unwavering support, and excellent advice. Deep down, they do so much for others because they yearn to be loved unconditionally and to have the love they give so freely come back to them.

Type twos can ignore their own needs yet tell someone else exactly what they think the other requires, from what to eat to whom to date, all while not following their own advice. A type two who does not feel needed can spiral, becoming passive-aggressive or even stern with words out of pain. Type twos will do whatever it takes to feel needed, because deep down they want to be loved and needed.

In conflict, type twos will become defensive and controlling when they do not feel loved or heard. Feeling rejected is their hot button. In communication, a partner of a type two should turn up the affection and reiterate his or her love for the type two even though they both may be in conflict. Take the time to listen and help remove any obstacles that may be keeping a type two from the self-care he or she has lacked while doing for others.

Denise, age forty-four, is a type two. She craves a lot of attention from Emanuel and can, in his words, be a full-time project. While working with Denise and Emanuel, I encouraged him to see her demands as a cry for help. When Denise was feeling overwhelmed, her sharp tongue would come out, causing damage to his ego and their intimacy. Emanuel has since taken up some of the heavy lifting by helping with the kids more. Denise now has more time for self-care and has taken up Pilates.

Type 3: The Achiever. Achievers are motivated communicators who learn from their mistakes. They can take direction and adapt to most situations. Type threes are ambitious and usually achieve most goals they set. They struggle with wanting to be the best at everything and feel the pressure to show a confident demeanor. A type three may appear one way but may actually be putting on an "everything is okay" face because of a deep-seated fear of failure. In relationships, type threes often act one way while feeling something else, leaving their partners in the dark. Type threes can struggle with who they are, and in times of despair seek recognition and admiration with self-promotional tactics. They seek to feel valued. When they feel valued, their confidence rises. They are born leaders and like to champion those around them when all is right in their world.

In conflict, they can get irritated quickly but still not be willing to admit what is bothering them. They do not like to fail and will become extremely embarrassed if they don't look like the self-assured person they portray when everything is going right for them. It is valuable for their partners to know not to approach them when they have a deadline. In communication, it is best not to interrupt them when they are focused on a task. If you want something, give them clear and concise examples of what you are asking for. Remind them of their value and show love and acceptance for how they approach things.

Type 4: The Individualist. This is a person who likes to be creative. Type fours can be demanding and temperamental, but they are romantics who see beauty in the world around them. Type fours are emotionally intense and driven. They have very high highs and the lowest lows. In search of value in themselves and the world around them, they set out on expeditions to find the meaning of life. They may continuously feel inadequate or as if something is missing within themselves, and may struggle with feelings of envy. Comparison to others leads to their constant need to create. Type fours have to watch that they don't go down a rabbit hole of looped thoughts involving comparison, shame, and emptiness. For type fours, it is best to focus on what they have and not what they desire.

In conflict, they are consumed by what others think of them. They can become moody, cold, and detached when they feel challenged or misunderstood. Partners should focus on reminding them of their uniqueness, creativity, and value. Type fours need to learn how to navigate their emotions and understand what is real to change their self-talk. In communication, when they are heard, they can be authentic, creative, and balanced. They need to know that they are indeed seen and loved. If you see a type four withdrawing, express your fears and emotions with them openly. Allow them to be emotional, and remind them how much you care for them and the beauty that you see in them. Being cherished is their universal desire.

Type 5: The Intellectual/Investigative Thinker. Type fives are smart, rational, and reserved. They can come off as arrogant or detached when feeling uninterested or distrustful. Type fives are usually hard workers and are always striving to know more. They can sometimes see the world as overwhelming and people as being too intrusive. When life gets too demanding, they can run for cover to try and conserve their energy for fear of giving away too much to the world. In basic terms, type fives can be know-it-alls and will not share their ideas or thoughts until they master the task at hand. As partners, they can come off as emotionally distant and private, which can cause issues because the other person longs to see vulnerabilities and commonalities.

In conflict, type fives can shut you down if they feel you have broken their trust, or if you expect too much of them with regard to obligations they are not ready for. They need time alone to gather their thoughts and develop empathy for what the other person is going through. In communication, their partners need to focus on the details. They need to tell them how much time they need to discuss an issue, then allow them the time they need alone to process what was said or asked of them. It is also a good thing to give type fives a heads-up on your agenda. They are at their best when they are in charge and have the room to pioneer the conversation.

Doug, age twenty-eight, says of his wife and business partner, who is a type five:

> She is a powerhouse. I have had to learn to jump on the bandwagon and just let her take the lead in work; however, in our intimate relationship, it has been more of a challenge. I have tried to show her that she can let go and even need me

sometimes. It has taken many years for her to trust me emotionally, not because I have done anything; it is just in her nature to do things on her own. I had to learn that is just how Kara is. By affirming my commitment to her, she has continued to grow and trust to let some things go. She is more at ease with our relationship. She tells me weekly when she is feeling depleted with our five kids, and I jump in to help carry the load. Understanding the Enneagram was a marriage-saver for us. Our communication and respect for one another have never been better.

Type 6: The Guardian. These people are as loyal and committed as they come. They are responsible, committed, reliable, and trustworthy. Type sixes are the epitome of a team player because of their abilities to bring people together. The unfortunate side of them is that they worry too much. They can become suspicious and have anxiety about the world around them. Assuming the worst is the hallmark of type sixes. They are just whom you want in your corner if a natural disaster were to hit, for they are planners, due to their need to have a sense of control in the face of the unknown. They crave predictability and safety and tend to focus on the bad stuff rather than the good stuff.

In conflict, type sixes can project their fears and insecurities as a means of protecting themselves. They can rely so much on fear that the what-ifs and doubts can wreak havoc on their relationships. When in conflict, type sixes can be so busy being anxious about the unknown that they may not see their partner's reality. They fear being lied to or abandoned and can become reactive when triggered. In communication, be clear and reassuring. Listen to their fears. Demonstrate empathy and show support without judgment.

Type 7: The Optimist. These are enthusiastic and entertaining extroverts who are eager, exciting, loyal, and bold. They thrive on having a good time and want to live life in a tremendous way. A type seven is good at bouncing back through emotional situations, hates to be bogged down with deep pain, and will attempt to avoid pain at all costs. Type sevens are escape artists who can disappear quickly when things are not going their way. They are in constant pursuit of the next thing, seeking innovation and new experiences at every turn. Because they want to avoid pain by removing painful barriers with escapism, it can be hard for relationship partners. They can struggle with commitment and boredom and become unreliable, choosing to have fun instead of staying to do the work needed to have relationship tranquility.

In conflict, they react when they feel limited or constrained. They get bored quickly by mundane tasks or asks. If they feel criticized, they will ghost you. It is crucial for type sevens to know that others don't think and process as quickly as they do. If you're a type seven, let your partner speak his or her peace before you take back control and deliver the issue more effectively and in a more timely fashion. If you're in a relationship with a type seven, be positive and complementary in your communication. Let your partner take control as much as possible. Be creative and let him or her have fun.

I am a type seven. My husband is a type one. The Enneagram has been an excellent tool for us in our marriage. As a seven, I can get bored very easily. I do process information very quickly, and for a time I even wondered if I had attention deficit disorder because of my lack of ability to stay engaged in some conversations. Here is an example of my husband and me discussing a scheduling issue for our kids. He will say something like, "I am going to need you to pick up Weston tomorrow." I hear it and immediately file it away on my to-do list, indicated by my nodding. Jon, however, being a perfectionistic type one, needs to confirm and reconfirm by stating or asking the same question in two or three different ways. I laugh at the thought of how this communication actually happens. For me, it's like communicating in slow motion. I have to slow down and confirm conclusively to keep the conversation going. He gets to feel confident in his plans, and I get to go off and dream. It works for us.

Type 8: The Challenger. Challengers are assertive, intense, confident, and powerful. Type eights can be quite hard to handle in a relationship, for they need to be in control every minute of every day. They are confrontational and, as the name says, challenging. On the one hand, they can do anything; on the other, they can be a bit too much for some people. At work, they can lead change. Although they have a hard exterior, inside they fear giving up their power. When challenged, they come out swinging. They act as if weakness is not something they ever feel. In relationships, intimacy is hard to share because of their lack of willingness to explore being vulnerable. Their core issue centers around never being allowed to feel weak or needy.

In conflict, they have an insatiable need to address wrongdoings. They try to have a spouse take responsibility for their actions. In communication with type eights, you will need to keep the specifics brief and stand your ground. They crave honesty and value directness. Ask clarifying questions. Remind them that they are safe to be vulnerable with you.

I had a friend in college who was an eight. She would go out to parties with us and start debates with all of the guys who were out with us. For her it was fun, but for many of them it was just too much. They saw her as the alpha male. She ended up marrying a guy who could hold his own. I saw them a few years ago at a party and watched as they argued about politics. They are very much in tune with their mental gymnastics. I was happy to see that she met her match in every sense of the word.

Type 9: The Peacemaker. These types like to mediate by reassuring and accommodating the people around them. Type nines are easygoing and agreeable. They are the opposite of eights in that they want everyone to get along without challenge. They can be passive in conflict and stubborn when it comes to sharing their point of view for fear of causing conflict. They are classic Avoiders and can leave others feeling unheard and frustrated by their complacency, which in turn causes the conflicts they try to avoid. Their core craving is to matter. When they feel like they matter, they are supportive and open. When they are ignored, they get tongue-tied trying to voice their opinions because frankly, they may not be sure what those opinions are.

In conflict, when their peace and harmony are interrupted or they feel taken advantage of, type nines will shut down. In communication, they need to see that conflict leads to resolution, that having feelings is normal. Their partners need to make them feel comfortable to share and promote resolution, and need to listen when they have ideas and encourage them to express their opinions.

One of the most significant breakdowns that I see in relationships is when two people don't take the time to understand where the other person truly is coming from. When we feel unheard, we shut down. When we shut down, we go inside our heads and try to rectify the situation. Self-talk is one of the areas where we can get into trouble. The narrative in our head can either keep us adequately aligned with loving strong or keep us in the weak zone.

To do relationships right, we have to know ourselves better. Learning how to communicate and handle conflict is a valuable part of the process. Now that you know your number, determine your partner's. Discover how you can love your partner more effectively based on personality type.

SELF-TALK

You now know by your personality type where your insecurities live. You know that your core issues can be sitting dormant inside, ready to be activated when you crave the messaging handed to you in childhood. In this part of the process, you have to shift your learned narrative to one of change and growth. To take power back in the dating world and beyond, your mind needs to be centered around your worth. Now it is time to dig into your self-talk. The way we speak to ourselves is powerful. Our internal dialogue can keep us stuck in ways we may never even understand. If we don't take the time to evaluate it, clean it up, and reframe it, we will continue to regress to our core messaging.

Remember when I said I was a personality type seven? Well, my internal fear messaging goes something like this: It is not okay to depend on others. When "the guy" left me, it woke up my inner child by confirming my biggest fears. I felt I was easily discarded and would always have to take care of myself physically, emotionally, and spiritually. It sounds foreign to me right now that my inner self-talk was so completely out of whack, but that is how it was for many of my early years. My narrative at the time was that I had to hold on to him for dear life because I would never again feel that way. My emotions and self-talk were very grandiose because I stayed in fear. To shift my thinking, I had to put it all out on the proverbial table. I decided to poke and prod at my fears enough to take away all of their power.

Because I am a writer, I decided first to start a journal about how I was feeling and write in it every single day. I poured out my fears and wrote about things I had never let see the light of day from my childhood, then I sat back and examined what I had written. I have to admit it was sad. By reading what I had written, I started to see that my little inner child was still running the show in my adult relationship. I took it a step further. At the local art store, I picked up a rainbow stack of sticky notes, and for the next seventy-two hours I wrote down every fear-based thought that I said to myself. I used a black Sharpie and stuck each admission on my wall. Soon my mirror and wall were covered with the fear-based self-talk I had been feeding myself since childhood.

When I had exhausted the process of writing, I sat with those sticky notes for another week. Everywhere I looked was fear. One day when I was on the phone with a girlfriend giving her a kick-ass pep talk, the irony of my not doing the same for myself hit me. The words were all around me, reminding me that the self I put out into the world was not the way I felt in my head. On the outside, I was highly functional, funny, and robust, yet on the inside, I was still a scared little girl. I decided that my exterior needed to match my interior, and the only way that would happen is if I believed in something better. Looking at the wall of fear, I took out a new Sharpie (hot pink) and changed the words. I replaced each doubt with a powerful message of worth. The one that sticks out in my head is "I am not lovable." I was and am lovable. I drew a line across the fear and replaced it with "I will be loved unconditionally with strength and conviction." Every time one of those fears would pop up in my brain, I would quickly shift to my new narratives. My life started to change in more ways than I could ever imagine. I was finally free to dream again. I felt unstoppable. I was indeed lovable.

Not all of the thoughts that go through our head are so serious, or so we may think. The times we say things and do things haphazardly also add up to harm. One of my clients, Cynthia, told me that every time she looks in a mirror, she pulls her shirt up and pats her stomach. She is a thin woman, so her patting her little tummy is not something you would think she would do. She confided that with each pat of her stomach, she would say to herself, "You need to lose that gut." I asked her to go home and write about it and see where her self-talk took her. This is what she told me: "After I rubbed my tummy yesterday, the next thing that popped in my head was, 'You have let yourself go. You are not the person you once were. You are weak.'" Cynthia could not believe what she had written down. Even while she was saying it out loud to me, she seemed overwhelmed and embarrassed. I reassured her that we all say things to ourselves that we would never say to someone else we love.

Another client of mine, Jenni, also had an epiphany while working through this part of the process. She was married to a man who was more of a leg man than a breast man. After she had their daughter, her breasts became big and saggy. When they did not perk back up after she lost the baby weight, she quit seeing herself as sexy. She had internalized that her breasts were not beautiful because her husband never touched them. The intimacy in her marriage went downhill, and a few years later, they divorced. When Jenni was back on the dating scene, she met a wonderful man who was a breast guy. It took her several months before she was comfortable enough for him to see her all the way naked, and even then she hesitated to remove her bra. Her self-talk had started to infringe on her new relationship without her even realizing it. I encouraged Jenni to carry a notebook with her and write down every negative thought that came into her mind. With Jenni's approval, I will share a few things she wrote here:

1. I need to lose fifteen pounds and quit eating like a pig.
2. My breasts look like two flat pancakes. I am not sexy.

3. I have got to start working out again to compete with these young women at the gym.
4. My breasts are the reason my ex lost his desire for me.
5. My left eye is droopy, and I need filler and Botox.
6. I am scared I am going to end up alone like my mom.
7. I think my new guy thinks my friend is sexier than me because she has fake breasts.
8. My C-section scar is a turnoff. I should have a plastic surgeon revise it.

The list went on and on. I know that these may seem superficial to many of you, but the negative thoughts go deeper than that. You see, Jenni's father was a plastic surgeon. His entire job was to nip and tuck women to make them look younger. He made her mother into someone unrecognizable before leaving her for a younger model. Jenni's mother said she could tell her father lost interest after her body changed from having kids. Jenni is a nine on the Enneagram. She craves peace. Her childhood messaging comes from her mother. She has inner conflict when she feels overlooked or ignored. Hence the negative self-talk that goes through her brain. Her new partner had to learn that Jenni needs to believe that she matters, that she should be encouraged to use her voice and admit how she feels. It turns out that Jenni's new man is much more turned on by her being comfortable asserting herself than he is by the size bra she wears.

EXERCISE: KEEP A THOUGHT JOURNAL

Jenni and I have two different stories, but our self-talk directly correlated to messaging from our childhoods. It was not working for either of us. The good news is, your inner dialogue can be easily changed by using positive affirmation repetition. Studies say it takes sixty-six days before a new behavior becomes automatic. For me, it took about a month. I call this part of the process "the reveal." I want you to keep a thought journal, as Jenni did, or you can use sticky notes, as I did. At the end of three days, I want you to highlight the negative comments in your journal. Sit with them for a few days and be mindful of what you say outwardly versus inwardly.

After your three days of writing down your negative self-talk, I want you to find a positive affirmation to counteract what you are saying to yourself. You will see that there are about five to ten damaging statements swirling around in that pretty little head of yours daily. Write your affirming statements about the self-talk you are determined to change. Then, for the next sixty-six days, put your new internal dialogue into practice. Note that change is not always straightforward or constant. But keep reaffirming yourself; once you get comfy with your new self-talk, share some of it with your council members. Ask them to call you out when they see you being harmful to yourself. Soon those berating messages will be a thing of the past.

By now you know I like a good song reference. Justin Timberlake wrote a song called "Mirrors" about the love he has for his wife, Jessica Biel, and how he learned that type of love by watching his grandparents, who were married for more than sixty years. In an interview about the song, Justin says: "One of the most valuable things in a relationship is being able to change and be individual continually, but look at the other side to the person that you're with and know that they're changing as well individually, but somehow you two can mirror each other and be the other half of the world that you both create."

Loving strong means having the ability to love and respect yourself while you and your partnership evolve. As individuals, as Justin said so eloquently, we are always growing, yet in many ways our core messaging stays the same. Finding the strength to love ourselves enough to accept the love that others give us takes a lot of resolve, love, and courage. By using the tools in this book, you will have a new methodology for getting the love you truly want. I am proud of you for doing this work. It may not be accessible at times, but the payoff can last a lifetime.

CHAPTER 9

RELATIONSHIP RESET: REPROGRAMMING YOUR HEAD AND HEART TO GIVE AND RECEIVE THE LOVE YOU DESERVE

Who you will become in your next relationship is based on the work you do today. I want you to feel good about all the time and effort you have put into this process. It is not for the faint of heart; it is, however, for the woman who is ready to take her control back. You are well on your way! By this point, you have spent a great deal of time thinking about your past and about your present relationships. We have discussed how your family of origin plays a big part in whom you pick and why you choose those people. You have also learned about your personality, communication, and conflict styles. All of this work is going to pay huge dividends when it comes to your next relationship or the one you are currently in. Self-awareness is the fundamental first step to taking your power back in relationships. Once you become aware of how you act and react in relationships, you can start to move into how and what you want to improve to get more of what you want in love.

We see memes every day that remind us to value ourselves as women. We are in a time when women are just starting to get a seat at the table at work and in our interpersonal relationships. As women, we are beginning to value not only who we are and what we have to say but also our worth. On the way to self-improvement, the biggest fumble I see with the women I work with is how they struggle with valuing themselves and, in turn, how they let other people treat them badly or devalue them. Women are taught from a very early age to be nurturers. We are accustomed to giving more than we receive. For many women, it comes down to just that. Women can still confuse what they have offered with their actual worth. Read that sentence again and put it in your memory bank. What this means is that women believe that if they keep giving in a relationship, they will ultimately get back the love they have given out so freely. When that love is not reciprocated, it has a direct line to their self-worth. They start to question themselves, their value, and their worth. When the giving becomes imbalanced between two people in a relationship, the person who is doing the taking can walk away scot-free, whereas the giver is left feeling defeated and wondering what happened. The giver wonders where he or she should have stopped giving or if he or she should try to give more. To make sure that you aren't giving too much of yourself away before figuring out if the other person is a good fit for you, I want to introduce you to the one thing that can help you more than any guru (not including me, of course), psychic, or dating app. Let me introduce you to your core values.

CORE VALUES

Think of core values as the extended version of tall, dark, and handsome. Core values should be added to your toolkit when you're picking a mate, for they are where the real value lies. Core values are defined by the fundamental beliefs a person has about life and how he or she chooses to go about it. They are the foundation for how we conduct ourselves out in the world, the guiding principles that help us understand what is right and what is wrong about our actions. A core value is a tool that you should use and refer back to continuously so you know if you are on the right path to your desired relationship destination. When we go off our chosen path or begin to question our worth, it is our core values that bring us back to the center. Those values also speak to us when a person we are in a relationship with does something to make us question our own significance.

Tall, dark, handsome, and loaded will not end well if the person underneath does not live in a way that is conducive to your value system. A woman accustomed to giving too much will inevitably fall back into her role of providing, and the relationship will begin to tip quickly toward the taker. Believe me, I see it all the time. Both men and women try to reimagine partners as the people they fantasize them to be, so they keep trying and giving, hoping to finally change the other person into what it is that they want and need them to be. Hormones and endorphins are the driving forces that bring two people together in the beginning. These hormones make us believe that anything is possible, but as we have discussed, when those feel-good hormones start to fade away, we are left with the core of the person.

A person's core values—not a bank account or good looks—keep the fires burning along the way to forever. By creating and sticking to your core values, you will be able to take the wheel in whom you pick as a long-term partner instead of just waiting for fate to do its job. Think about what you want in a future partner—the real stuff, such as what kind of person he or she really is. How does this person treat others? Does this person respect himself or herself and the people around them? Do you trust that this person will do the right thing even when you are not there? Does this person make you feel weak or secure?

The version of yourself the other person brings out in you should be a telltale sign. When we love strong, we use core values to talk about what we love about someone. We are proud of who this person and use descriptive words such as "honest," "respectful," and "patient." When we are working against the universe, we often rely on peripheral things such as looks, money, and stature. Those external characteristics can take you only so far.

Core values, like the other things we've discussed, are instilled in us by our parents and early experiences in the world. We learn by listening and watching to see what our parents value. We also pick up lessons that help dictate the changes we wish to see in our own adult lives. We can choose to implement our parents' values and goals or redefine ourselves based on what we feel their values lacked. For instance, my mother, as we have discussed, taught me to be tough. In many ways, she taught me to depend on myself so much so that I feared to be vulnerable with others. A core value my mother has is trust, but she did not necessarily always trust others or expect others to trust. She valued it, but did she live it?

It took a few heartbreaks for her to value trust in herself and others. I watched how those experiences shaped her, and I started to make adjustments in my own beliefs. With core values, you have to walk the walk, not just talk the talk. What you say must always be in line with what you do, because if we don't have our standards, how will others know what we value? When our values and actions are not working in tandem, we expose ourselves to hurt. This can be a rite of passage, but if a lesson is not learned when someone else hurts us, we will presumably be hurt again.

Most breakups happen when the newness wears off in the early stages of a relationship, revealing what a person is made of. If a couple's core values are not in alignment, sooner or later one person will let the other down. In weak love, the more vulnerable person will start giving in, setting aside their own needs or beliefs to get realigned with their partner. If there are fundamental differences in belief systems, a solid foundation cannot be set. A back-and-forth will commence, with each person trying to convince the other to believe in his or her way. In the end, the giver will keep giving, and the taker will keep taking. It is a slippery slope, and one that someone is bound to get hurt by. We must remember our worth and value ourselves enough to attract those who will do the same and love us strongly.

Casey, age thirty-eight, was just out of her marriage when Chris showed up like a knight in shining armor, or so she thought. Her marriage had been doomed from the start. Her then husband was an up-and-coming plastic surgeon in Los Angeles. He was invited to all of the major parties and operated on some of the biggest stars around. He was mingling with Hollywood's elite and staying out to all hours of the night, leaving Casey at home to take care of their toddler. She found out about his many infidelities after one of the nurses in his office confided in Casey before quitting her job. Casey tried to forgive him, and they even went to couples' therapy for a while, but in the end, he just wanted to replace her with a younger, more exciting version. Reeling from her divorce, she looked both consciously and subconsciously for a man who could meet some of the expensive "needs" she had become accustomed to—she believed that money and stature would make her happy.

Enter Chris, who was a good-looking, flashy man in his late forties. He seemed to have it all: money, looks, and a desire to settle down. Casey jumped in fast. Soon she and her son were a fixture at Chris' home. Casey started playing house and throwing lavish parties. It was one of Casey's friends, Charlotte, who first noticed that something about Chris was just a bit too good to be true. Specifically, how he made his money. She brought this up with Casey, asking her to dig a little deeper into what he was all about; however, Casey did not want to come off her high. She wanted to believe everything was on the up and up, and refused to ask Chris about his questionable finances. Charlotte referred to Chris as a poser. She said he was a social climber, and she believed that Casey refused to see it. To Charlotte, Chris was a carbon copy of Casey's ex-husband, minus the Harvard education.

Fast-forward two years. Chris' house had been foreclosed on. His business partner sued him for stealing money, and he had broken things off with Casey, leaving her devastated. Casey spent the next year going through my process. In the end, she discovered that there had been many red flags for Casey with both her ex-husband and Chris. She chose to go with the outer package versus looking at both men's inner core values, or lack thereof. Casey had some unresolved issues that took her committing to my methodology for her to uncover. The core values we focused on were trust, respect, dependability, honesty, and consistency.

In reviewing her time with Chris, she recognized that his lack of consistency, reliability, and trust was evident from the get-go in how he treated his business partner. She confided knowing that he had moved money from a few accounts unbeknownst to his partner, leaving that little voice inside of her yelling to get her attention. She had ignored so many things because she just wanted to be loved. Her ex-husband's inconsistency and lack of honesty had driven her to become someone she could hardly recognize. In the end, her morals and core values regrounded her. She now has a solid love in her life. Casey has been dating her boyfriend, Jared, for just over a year. He is kind, considerate, and trustworthy. They are in perfect alignment.

I get it. Everyone wants to be loved, but weak love will reduce the chances of your getting what you need. Relationships built on a weak foundation do not have the strength to weather the storms in life. They can crumble on a moment's notice, leaving you to pick up all of the broken pieces. My goal is to stop you from any missteps by giving you a chance to strengthen your core.

Remember Suzanne from chapter one? She was the young lady who came to all of my speaking engagements and never said a word until one day when she unloaded on me about her unhealthy relationship patterns. She had been led to believe that a good man is hard to find.

Well, she sent me a text a few months ago to tell me she had met the one. When I called to check in, she told me all about her new guy. She talked about his core values and how she had learned so much about herself before meeting him. She thanked me for helping her before hanging up. Two days later, I got a frantic text from her telling me her new beau may be cheating on her. Because trust is one of her core values, something had told her to check his phone. Upon doing so, she saw some texts between him and an ex-girlfriend. She called me immediately and told me all that had transpired. My heart ached for her as I listened to the story. I gave her my feedback and waited to see what she would do. To my surprise, she completely kept her cool. She told her boyfriend that she would leave his phone in the mailbox to pick up and they could talk in a day or two when she had time to clear her head. This was a *huge* step for Suzanne, as she had always lacked impulse control. I spoke with her a few days later. Gone was the insecure girl who looked for my approval in her every step. She had been replaced by a woman who knew her worth. She ended up choosing to give her new beau another chance. She is trusting herself for the first time in years—and that, my friends, is progress.

Suzanne's core values are fairness, open-mindedness, trust, responsiveness, and intuition. She finally feels she is in a place where she can see both sides of the situation. She is open to where the relationship can go but has made it absolutely clear what she will and will not deal with moving forward. Understanding your value does not mean that human mistakes will not challenge you. What it offers is the ability to trust yourself to make the best decisions you can make. I learned that firsthand during my long-distance relationship with my future husband.

Jon and I dated for about a year in Atlanta before his coaching career took him to a few different states over the next five years. There were times when our schedules did not align and we couldn't see each other. Many times we went weeks, if not months, without seeing each other. We were both still growing individually, and that meant there were some breaks along the way to our forever. Most of my friends did not understand his schedule. He was either coaching, practicing, or recruiting every single weekend during the years he coached. His commitment to coaching meant that his promise to me came second for a time in our lives. He missed monumental moments like my best friend's wedding, helping me move into my first house, and too many holidays to count. A guy friend of mine once said to me, "You do know he is playing you. I am sure a good-looking guy like him on a college campus surrounded by adoring fans is bound to slip up. I can promise you he is cheating on you." The funny thing is, it did not bother me. I had so much trust in what we had that I did not waiver.

When I look back on that time in our lives, I feel nothing but pride. The reason? I knew who he was and what he stood for. He was always honest with me, even sometimes to a fault. He told me when he was unsure and confided in his perceived selfishness when he could not give me what I may have wanted. It was in those moments that I knew he valued me, respected me, and accepted when I needed to go on my separate way. Believe it or not, I almost married another guy during one of those breaks in our relationship. That other guy checked off everything on my list except for being optimistic, fun, and willing to take risks.

To put it bluntly, he was predictable and safe. He wanted a commitment and promised to give me the life I longed for; however, his lack of ambition and unwillingness to take risks was a real snore and soon left me feeling the void of Jon. I longed for our real conversations and mutual fire for chasing our dreams. I decided that I wanted to take a risk with Jon, and everything else fell nicely into place. We married less than a year later. Our courtship lasted through three states, eight years, another man, and countless ultimatums. Why? I think our values lined up, and they still do today.

EXERCISE: IDENTIFY YOUR CORE VALUES

All of these stories should have you wondering about your core values. When you think of your relationships that have weathered many storms, I am sure that it is your aligned values that can take most of the credit. To clarify where you stand and what your beliefs are, let's focus on your core values.

In this exercise, read through the list below and circle ten to fifteen words that resonate with you.

Acceptance	Fairness	Optimism
Accountability	Family	Originality
Advocacy	Flexibility	Passion
Affection	Forgiveness	Patience
Agility	Friendship	Peacefulness
Ambition	Fulfillment	Persistence
Attentiveness	Fun	Playfulness
Balance	Generosity	Power
Boldness	Grace	Pragmatism
Bravery	Happiness	Privacy
Calmness	Honorability	Protection
Caring	Humility	Realness
Charity	Inclusivity	Respect
Collaboration	Independence	Responsibility
Commitment	Inspiration	Risk-taking
Compassion	Integrity	Sacrifice
Confidence	Justice	Safety
Consistency	Kindness	Security
Credibility	Leadership	Self-motivation
Decisiveness	Level-headedness	Stability
Dependability	Love	Support
Empathy	Loyalty	Transparency
Empowerment	Making a difference	Trustworthiness
Encouragement	Mindfulness	
Ethics	Open-mindedness	

Now, take the circled words and narrow them down to the five that speak specifically to who you are and what you value as a person. You may go back and forth on a few. You may even have more than five. Highlight them and sit with them for a few days. Think about ways you would describe yourself or how others have described you. Soon you will have clarity on your core values. I can tell you without question that if you zero in on these traits for yourself and the ones you value in your potential partner, you can never go wrong. Sure, people are going to let you down, but if you focus on these values as your driving force, you will never give too much of yourself to the wrong person again.

Nicole and I went round and round in this part of the process when I was working with her. She was stuck on two men. Both were named Scott, believe it or not. One was husband material, and the other guy was a loser (to be frank); however, the loser was good in bed and highly seductive. Nicole kept going back and forth between the two men. She was determined that one of them was "the one." Then Nicole chose her five traits, and the top one was honesty. I asked her to take some much-needed time to be alone without either guy to try to understand herself more without the distraction of both men. After some trial-and-error, she finally listened. She told bad Scott she wanted to take a break to work on herself. He did not put up a fight. A week or two later, she panicked and called him. They met for a drink, and Scott went into seduction mode. Drinks led to their going back to her house, and just before anything significant could go down, she caught him on his phone texting another girl.

Nicole went through her checklist of required traits. Honesty was one of her top characteristics. She asked herself, "Does he have this trait?" The answer was a resounding no, and with that, she had her answer.

I can tell you with confidence that if you go by your selected values, they will have your back every time. Now that you have decided on your core values and the ones you want in another person, it is time to move on from self-awareness to self-improvement—the good stuff!

FORGIVENESS

We have all seen the friend who can give out the best advice but never take the information herself. Maybe you have even been that person. We can know what we want to do, and we can be aware of where we may have gotten stuck in the past, yet still lack the know-how for how to improve moving forward. One of the most critical parts of self-improvement is forgiveness. Learning to forgive ourselves is key to loving strong.

For me, and for my clients, the biggest part of the process is forgiveness. Forgiving yourself is a large hill to climb, whether you are working through a minor infraction (such as sleeping with an ex-lover) or a major obstacle (such as staying in an abusive relationship for far too long). No matter how big or how small you deem the issue, the steps you will need to take to forgive yourself will look and feel the same. Forgiveness forces us to let our past hurt die. You have to decide to let go of the idea of someone or something that did not go as we planned. You have to be willing to let it all go. If you can't let go, you will remain a victim in that situation. You either will become detached from yourself to "cope," or you will dance with anger. Both states will keep you stuck in a lose-lose situation. The mental gymnastics take a toll that will keep you chained to the situation or paralyzed in fear. To untether yourself from either state, you have to be willing to forgive. Forgiveness is the highest form of love we can have for ourselves. It takes empathy and compassion to take these necessary steps to heal.

EXERCISE: FORGIVE YOURSELF

First, write down what you need to forgive yourself for.

I forgive myself for

_____

_____

_____

_____.

Next think about what you have missed out on during your self-imposed purgatory. What has it stopped you from doing?

The anger and/or detachment I have felt have stopped me from being able to

_____

_____

_____.

Here are a few tips to help you through the process.

1. Going through this process is allowing you not only to focus on your emotions but to feel them. You are well on your way to processing all of the reasons you may have gotten stuck, hurt, or given up in love. You will write down all of these in "the 3 C's" relationship contract below.
2. By having awareness and your relationship council, you can now acknowledge your mistakes. Admitting faults or missteps takes away their power. By saying things out loud, you will find the freedom you need to forgive your past self. We do better when we know better. I remember feeling major embarrassment about being divorced

at such a young age. To me, divorce was like a scarlet letter that told the world I had no earthly idea what I was
doing. The imprint that mistake made on me was that
I could not trust myself to make the right decisions. I
had to forgive myself for my divorce. Then I had to start
talking about it. When I started working my divorce into
conversations, the weight it had in my mind and on my
heart faded away. It had held me back from being myself
fully, and for a time, I had detached from many of the
things that brought me joy in my life. The new narrative I replaced it with was that I loved and respected
myself enough to walk away. I wished my ex love and
light, and forgave myself for hurting him. My freedom
was restored, and my search for strong love could begin.

3. We can learn from our mistakes, just as I did in my
divorce. Remind yourself out loud that you did the best
you could with the tools and experiences you had at the
time. Now, with my process, you can have an algorithm
for your dating life. You will soon know where you get
triggered, why, and what to do about it.

4. Don't allow the mistake to fester in your brain. Say your
mistake out loud. Write down or discuss your feelings
around the error. Then put the mistake in a timeout.
Meaning, give it only the time you need to recognize
what it taught you and how that lesson can help you
in the future. If your inner critic starts to ruminate on
what happened, again put it in a timeout. Give the mistake a short platform of fifteen to twenty minutes of dis-
cussion, then push yourself to shut it down. The idea
is to learn the lesson, not to beat yourself up about the
mistake itself.

5. Be your own cheerleader. Write down the vital attributes you admire in yourself, like your core values. Say them out loud when talking through any issues that might have sidelined you in the past. For example, if you walked away from a relationship but recently gave in to calling your ex, you may say something like this: "Being honest about my feelings is something I value. I wanted to tell my ex about why I called him the other night after a few cocktails. I let him know that I had a moment of missing him, but upon reflection know our breakup is for the best. I am proud of myself for being upfront and honest." If you want to take it a step further, get out a piece of paper and, with your dominant hand, write down the statements your inner critic is saying about you and your mistake. Next, put the pen in your nondominant hand and write a compassionate, empathetic rebuttal to yourself. Using the opposite hand exercises the brain. It allows the mind to forge new neural connections versus going back to what it already knows.

6. Have clarity around your need to self-improve. Do you want or need to make amends with yourself or another person to forgive yourself? Sometimes saying you are sorry and leading with love can get you over the hump in a situation. Clearing the air is a necessary part of the process for forgiving both yourself and others. If you are still stuck on what to do, ask yourself what you would tell a loved one to do in that same situation. It can also help to ask a trusted friend to role-play with you. Let the friend be you, and you be the advice-giver. Listen to the advice you offer your friend, and take it to heart yourself.

7. Give yourself time to process it all. Breaking unhealthy patterns and learning new ways to cope takes time.

Celebrate the moments when you do well, and don't belabor any regressions. You are healing, and that is what is most important.

8. Don't be afraid to ask for help. Let others in, but if you realize you are expecting too much from them, it may be time to seek the help of a coach or therapist to help you work through your healing.

Identifying what you are feeling is a significant step in awareness. Learning new ways to cope and forgive ourselves is where the real improvement happens. Another significant aspect of improvement is learning to understand our strengths, weaknesses, feelings, fears, and values, as well as how they all affect the people we are in relationships with. To improve, we have to hold ourselves accountable for our actions and reactions. Deciding exactly where you want to grow in your relationships is an excellent way to self-manage yourself versus projecting those issues onto other people to manage. In a sense, we are all on autopilot in our relationships. To self-manage, we have to form new non-habitual behaviors that require us to slow down, consider other people's feelings, make and consider choices, and demonstrate a new behavior that aligns with our original choices. Just like dieting, it takes a considerable amount of effort and willpower to self-improve, but it can be learned. It is time to get excited. Once you begin the process of self-improvement, new opportunities and growth will flow into your love life.

THE 3 C'S

A relationship contract with yourself might seem corny, but I promise you it is useful. I call the contract "the 3 C's." The *C*s stand for "clarity, curation, and commitment." I will identify what each *C* means and then ask you to define each one for yourself.

> **Clarity:** You need a clear purpose around what type of relationship you will have with yourself and a future romantic partner. The clearer you are on what you want, the less room there will be for assumptions. Intent allows you to feel confident about where you are going and how you plan to get there. By sharing your intention, you offer an understanding to your future partner on why the relationship matters to you, how you like to build a foundation, and what you will do when difficulties arise as you grow closer.
>
> First clarify your core values and the values you want in a partner, then fill in the blanks for the sentences that follow.

My Core Values	My Partner's Core Values
1.	1.
2.	2.
3.	3.
4.	4.
5.	5.

My intentions for my next relationship are:

_____

_____.

The foundation I am looking for will be built on:

_____

_____.

To get ready to handle difficulties that may arise, I will continue to work on

_____

_____.

by doing the following for myself:

_____

_____.

Initial here:

_____

Curation: Have you ever put your heart and soul into loving another person only to see the fruits of your labor be enjoyed in the person's next relationship? I know, it can be frustrating. To make sure you are curating the right relationship, it is vital to understand what loving strong will look like for you in your next relationship. What will the other person offer, and what will you offer in return? Weak love can take on many forms and take too much of our most valued resource, which is our heart. When we love weakly, the relationship is more transactional. One or both parties put in minimal effort, and the requirements are low.

Then there are the weak relationships that start seemingly strong, with shared goals, mutual respect, and expectations. Although these relationships may start with a bang, over time it becomes apparent that a stronger, more profound love is not going to flourish, as one or both people quit putting in the effort needed for it to grow.

Then there is the transformational love that allows both people to grow together and curate the relationship, helping it become strong love. This happens when there are mutual goals and respect, when we enable each person to be nurtured as well as vulnerable when needed. In this love, we are open to another's opinions, desires, values, and needs. We hold the other person to a higher standard, even when it can be difficult. We love unconditionally and are the purest form of our best self.

If you are ready for strong, transformational love, initial here _____.

Commitment: Having a great relationship with yourself may not happen overnight, but if you commit to putting yourself, your healing, and your needs first it can and will occur. To commit to loving someone, you must first love yourself. It is okay to have bouts of discord or even sometimes to let yourself down; however, with a real commitment to loving yourself, you realize that you can and will fall; it is how you get back up that matters. An intention is a powerful tool.

For the next six months, I want you to commit to loving strong. Whatever in your life is being held together by a weak thread, let it go. Let go of a weak boss, a weak lover, or uncertain intentions. Commit to the next six months of magic. Let go whatever aspect of your life

that does not yield strong love, to make room
for the real deal.

Initial here if you are ready to commit to
loving who you are, what you want, and whom
you give yourself to: _____.

Wow, girl, you are ready now! You have signed the contract
and are prepared for your relationship reset. Throughout this
entire process, you have worked on reprogramming your heart
and your head to be ready to receive big, magical, strong love.

TAKING THE LOVE-STRONG LEAP

Many people are great at giving love, but sometimes being able
to receive love can be a challenge. It goes back to feeling worthy
of it all. In the book *The Big Leap*, author Gay Hendricks talks
about the "Upper Limit Problem." We all feel as though we have
an upper limit we can reach, and once we have gotten there, we
sabotage ourselves, believing we can't possibly have even more.
An example of this is thinking that you can't love again after
divorce because you initiated the divorce and don't deserve to
love more. Another example would be finally reaching the pinna-
cle of your career, then sabotaging yourself by worrying that you
are not good enough to excel in it and to maybe even go places
you'd never dreamed of.

There are a few fundamental reasons we all may have an
upper limit in strong love. One is feeling unworthy. We fear
we don't deserve magical love and true jaw-dropping happiness. Another obstacle is feeling that we are undeserving of joy
because we have been disloyal or left people behind who have
been there for us in the past. We pull back from going for it
because fear tells us we may end up alone. Another reason we

may hold back in loving strong is fear of outshining others or getting what others can't seem to grasp. To take the strong-love leap, you have to believe that you can and will have that big, magical love. The more you see that vision of yourself, and the more you practice being the best version of yourself, the closer you will get to your ultimate goal.

You have to believe to receive.

What I am imploring you to do is to shake off any belief system that you may have that you are not worthy of strong love. Anytime that feeling of unworthiness or doubt begins to surface, I want you to shake it off. Seriously, if your ego is trying to mess with you right now, shake it off. Stand up and jump around and say out loud, "I am worthy of loving strong! Ego, take a hike. I have big, magical love coming my way!"

To believe, you have to know that who you are today is enough. You are enough. Start to become more open to receiving. See it in the kind gesture from the elderly man who may have held the door open for you, or find it in a child's smile. Empower others to give to you as you openly receive what is coming to you. Take notice and you will start to see all of the ways the universe is jumping in to help you in your new flow of receiving. Practice gratitude for all of the love you are accepting and try to give back without expectations. Believe in balance and know that you are meant to both give and receive. Be ready and willing to do both.

CHAPTER 10

TAKE YOUR POWER BACK: CHANGE YOUR NARRATIVE, CHANGE YOUR LIFE

I have a client who is a successful businesswoman, a mother, and an overall fabulous human being. She knows her worth and dates accordingly...for the most part. There is a part of her that tends to be so emotionally mature that without knowing it, she can still give up her power. It happens. Taking your power back doesn't always happen on autopilot. What taking your power back is about is taking the time to evaluate how you are feeling on a routine basis in any given situation. If and when you feel the power shift, stop and take inventory. As you have learned in this process, the real problem is not always about what is right in front of you but rather your reaction to it.

Here is a little more backstory on my client. She has been dating a man off and on for two years. He is in the last year of his fellowship to become a surgeon, a second career he took on in his mid-twenties after law school. He has promised her that things will get better, yet she remains on the back burner or even off the stove altogether. He works crazy hours, sleeps when he is off, and does not put much effort into their relationship. My client wants to be supportive, but she is becoming more and more bored in the relationship. The mature part of her wants to continue to give him the space he needs to follow his dreams; however, another part is screaming for attention and reassurance. What should she do?

I have another client, a man. (Yes, I work with plenty of men, too.) He has been engaged to his fiancée for over a year, yet is unsure if he wants to get married. They are polar opposites. He likes to lounge around on the weekends and see where the day takes him, whereas she likes to have a plan and traipse all over the Colorado mountains checking off her to-dos. He has been withdrawing and feeling suffocated by all of the constant planning in his life. After talking to me and everyone else who would listen about his situation, he still felt stifled. Tired of feeling stuck, he called off the engagement to give himself some room to breathe. Now, he feels like he might have screwed up his life. He says he feels like he let everyone down and is a bad person. He keeps referring to himself as a "disaster." He has convinced himself that everyone is judging him and that her family and friends hate him. What should he do?

Though both stories may seem polar opposites, both clients have shifted the narrative to accommodate the significant others in their lives. Both people have given away their power without even realizing it. By giving away their power, they have also made themselves second fiddle. Sacrifice is a significant and sometimes noble part of a relationship. We are all tasked sometimes in our lives with forgoing our own needs for a time to help our loved one reach a dream or deal with a life circumstance. Those times are what bring people closer in many cases; however, if we don't maintain our worth, we can and will give up our power without even knowing it.

Our personal narratives are made up of the stories we tell ourselves as a result of our histories, our experiences, and the decisions we have made in our lives. Our belief systems directly affect our behaviors. My female client described above may believe she is not important enough to ask for more. My male client may think he is lazy or unworthy of someone who is more self-motivated than he wants to be. Whatever the case, they are both friendly, loving human beings who deserve to have the love they want. So, what gives?

What gives is their belief systems. They—and you—are in fact good enough and are capable and worthy of loving strong. By clinging to excuses that we are not enough, we prevent ourselves from being able to get the love we so desperately want because we are so busy telling ourselves we can't have it. Who has time for that nonsense any longer? Surely, not you.

Throughout this process, you have identified all of the false advertising you may have been listening to in your head. To change your narrative in any given situation, you first have to pinpoint the narrative you need and want to change. In my male client's case, he wanted to quit seeing himself as a disaster and an overall loser for hurting his fiancée. First, he had to stop putting himself down. Those defining statements were not helping him and were keeping him stuck in a victim mentality.

Next, he had to catch himself in the act. When those words or that narrative came into his head or out of his mouth, he had to stop cold turkey and negate the narrative by saying something else out loud that would bring him back to neutral. An example we worked on was, "I took a break to understand better why I was feeling some of the feelings I was feeling. I did it out of love for us both." By bringing it back to neutral, he was writing a new narrative and taking back his control.

My female client had to change her narrative from "I am scared to rock the boat because I may come across like an emotional basket case for asking for reassurance once again" to one that considered her emotional needs. Her new narrative was, "I have needs just like every other woman out there. I am only asking to feel more like a partner. It is okay to ask for what I need."

POWER-BALANCE PROHIBITIONS

This entire process is teaching you to expect big, magical, strong love. As a reminder about everything we have discussed and you have processed, here are eight ways you may have given your power away in the past. You want to avoid them to keep an even balance of power in your relationships.

1. You allowed someone else's opinion guilt-trip you. No, ma'am. This is not allowed anymore. Don't give your power away based on someone else's issue. You know your worth. Everything else is about the other person, not you.

2. You didn't stick to your boundaries. By allowing someone else to dictate what works for you, you started to give up your power. Limits are set to teach people how to treat us. A big sign of a boundary power struggle is resentment. If you feel resentful, you have most likely let someone cross your boundaries.

3. You held on to the past. Meaning, you held on to anger, which prevented you from moving on to what you wanted to feel. You have the choice to let go of people and things that no longer serve you. If you are holding

on to those things, you are depleting your mental capac-
ity to let the good come in.

4. You reacted to what others were serving. Don't let toxic
people provoke you or slow your roll. Stay in tune with
your own self-worth and core values. Rise above the
fray and leave the drama for someone else. You have
magic to capture.

5. You changed your goals based on someone else's plan.
You know what you want now more than ever. Don't let
a heartbreak derail you from the real you. Stick to your
dreams. The right person will help you achieve them.

6. You kept trying to change someone's opinion of you.
Don't be tempted to alter or contort yourself into someone else's vision of you. Stay your course. The weak loves
will fall back, and the strong ones will lean in.

7. You let your inner conflict win. If you are stuck, it
is because you don't want to change your narrative.
Remember: Your internal conflict is not in control of
you. It is a tool to recognize your starting-off point. You
decide your destination.

8. You took responsibility for other people's actions. Your
responsibilities are your words, behaviors, actions, and
mistakes, and the consequences of them all. You are not
responsible for:

- Other people's actions.
- Other people's words.
- Other people's mistakes.
- Other people's beliefs.
- Other people's core values.
- Other people's ideas.
- Other people's consequences to their actions.

Not that I think any of you are going to give your power away moving forward, but just in case you start to stumble, refer back to this list. Regroup and get on with doing you!

Janelle, age twenty-three, had a full-circle moment when working to change her narrative, change her life, and take her power back. She had lived with a guy, Kam, since high school, and he had an escalating drinking problem. Over time a power shift had happened, and Janelle tried to stop doing things that would trigger Kam. His loss of job opportunities became her problem because she did not want to move out of state to follow him down a career path to nowhere after he had burned too many bridges at home. His lack of sexual desire became her problem because she "complained" too much and made him not want to have sex. Janelle, finally at her wit's end, moved out.

His family then freaked out because now he was their problem. They all chose Kam's side and continued to enable him as Janelle once had. When Kam asked her to move back in, she gave him an ultimatum, saying he needed to get help. He went into a thirty-day rehab facility, and the tides seemed to be turning in their favor. Then about a month into his sobriety, he went to a wedding and got bombed. Janelle got him home safely, called his father, and left later that night, moving out for the final time.

When I started working with Janelle, she was stuck on what everyone thought of her in his family. Kam had told everyone that the reason his drinking had gotten worse was her refusal to move away for the job opportunity. He omitted the fact that the job had a ninety-day probation period. Janelle knew in her heart of hearts he would most likely not be able to stay clean for those three months. Kam was playing both sides and not taking responsibility for his shortcomings. Janelle was still in love with the guy she had met all those years ago who was full of dreams and testosterone. She had given away her power by trying to right all of the "wrongs" he kept pointing out about her.

To take her power back, Janelle asked him to work on himself while she moved home and did the same. She keeps the eight Power-Balance Prohibitions on her phone and reads them every time he tries to project his anger and resentment onto her. They are now in what Janelle calls a friendship phase. She still loves him but knows she deserves better. She is contemplating spending a year traveling all over Europe, a dream she had put off for Kam.

The key for Janelle was to get out of a reactive mode and become proactive. Being proactive involves learning how to avert problems by planning ahead. By anticipating and planning the future you want, you can take responsibility, control your actions, and focus on the good stuff.

EXERCISE: WRITE YOUR FULL-CIRCLE STORY

Now take out your journal; you're going to write down your full-circle story. A full-circle tale comes from the heart and should recap what you've learned, how you will use it, and what you feel will come from all that you have learned. Look back through each chapter, jot down some notes from each exercise and put everything into story form. The story will have three parts: your past, your present, and your future, just as the outline of the book is set up. What are your biggest takeaways from what you've learned concerning your past? How will those things you have learned be used in your present or future relationships? Will you pay closer attention to whom you choose or how you deal with conflict? Last, write about the future you see for yourself. How does it look? What does it feel like? What possibilities does your future hold?

EXERCISE: MEET YOUR FUTURE SELF

One of my favorite exercises that I like to do with my clients is called Meet Your Future Self. Read it through now and then download it from my website. Or grab someone from your relationship council to walk you through the practice. Once you get all of the logistics straight, we will get started.

Go to a spot where you can't be disturbed. Turn off your phone and any other distractions, such as the TV or computer. Turn down the lights and allow yourself to get into a meditative state. You are going to glance into your future.

1. Close your eyes. We are going to go on a little journey together.
2. Relax your body, starting with your toes. Slowly allow each part of your body to go limp and weightless.
3. Relax your eyes and mouth, unclenching your jaw.
4. Relax your forehead and unfurrow your brow.
5. Visualize a beam of soft light coming from the center of your heart. Imagine the light beaming from you off into the sky, past the clouds and into the quietness of space.
6. Visualize your spirit following the beam on its journey.
7. Let yourself feel your weightless body following the beam up and through the clouds. Once you get to what looks like the end of the beam, you will notice a small loop taking you back into the direction of the earth. You are floating effortlessly.
8. As you are coming back down, imagine yourself twenty years into the future.
9. Come to your future house. What does it look like? Describe how it makes you feel. What do you notice? What do you like?

10. Glide up to the front door and quietly knock. As the door opens, see your future self.
11. Ask your future self if she would be willing to share some insight with you.
12. Ask her what she likes about her life. Ask her the three most important things she remembers about the previous twenty years.
13. Find out what her spirit needs to know to get her from her present life to her future self.
14. Ask what worked and what did not work to get her to this place.
15. Ask what the biggest lesson she needs to learn now is.
16. Ask her to describe her love status. Is she married? Happily? If so, what does he or she look like? What does she cherish about her partner? How does this person make her feel?
17. Once the sharing is over, thank your future self and let her float back in the direction of the light.
18. Slowly come back to where you are today, allowing yourself as much time as you need.
19. Count from ten down to one, slowly allowing yourself to come back to the present.
20. Open your eyes.

The future-self exercise is meant to allow you to see that you have a much bigger capability in love than what you may be thinking today. Write down what you learned about your future self. Describe every detail and allow yourself to start imagining the possibilities.

LIMITING BELIEFS

Let me play devil's advocate here. You may have thought that the future-self exercise is a little corny, or perhaps it was right up your alley because you love that kind of stuff. Either way, beware what wants to steal your love joy when you are attempting to dream about your future possibilities: your limiting beliefs. A limiting belief is like that loud aunt who drinks too much at Christmas. She has been around since childhood, and everyone tolerates her, but the question is, do you have to? Limiting beliefs come from overwhelming emotions that have stunted us in some ways from—yes, you guessed it—childhood. They stop us dead in our tracks both consciously and subconsciously, keeping us from actually living in the here and now. They constrain us and can impoverish our emotional lives. To signal when a limiting belief is coming, here are a few key phrases that may begin one:

- "I can't"
- "I must"
- "I am"
- "I am not"
- "I never"
- "I am never"

I hear limiting beliefs every single day from clients who are petrified to change their narrative. Experiences can cause us to form limiting beliefs. At one point in our lives, those experiences and ideas may have kept us safe or out of harm's way. An example could be that as a child, you jumped out of a tree and broke your leg; now, as an adult, you believe that taking any risk will result in personal injury, so you refuse to try new things for fear of getting hurt.

Limiting beliefs also come from what we are taught formally and informally. As we learn and grow, we are heavily influenced by those around us. Over time we can absorb other people's limited beliefs merely by being around them. A simple example may be that if you have a parent who is a die-hard USC fan, you too might be a big fan. This may not seem like a big deal at all; however, it can go deeper. Being told what is right and wrong or that we are good only at certain things can stop us from living out our heart's desires.

An example may be a couple who own a law firm and expect their son also to want to practice law. Well, how about if he aspires to do something in the arts, such as acting, and his parents tell him he will never make a living in acting. Will that limiting belief stop him or propel him?

Most limiting beliefs are based in fear. Worrying about making a wrong decision, wasting time, or being criticized can also stop us from going forward in love. I have a client who continually tells me she will never meet any good man. She refers back to her bad decision-making always and berates herself for continuing to fall for the wrong men. When I try to redirect her, she goes quiet and says she is just not as lucky as her other friends and is destined to be alone. Her mother has been unhappily married for decades, and she has seen and heard the outcome of her mother's bad decisions. Those limiting beliefs have sent her right into the arms of a married man.

So, if and when one of your limiting beliefs come up, what should you do? Let's say you are just out of a breakup and want to believe in finding love again, like my client above. First, you have to tackle what limiting belief is stopping you. Did it come from a specific wrong decision?

I will use the married-man scenario to guide you through my client's limiting belief. My client made a wrong decision. The source of her limiting belief is her mother. It goes back to her mother's ingraining in her that men are not always good.

Therefore, my client had settled for the quintessential "bad guy." For her to change her limiting belief and overall victim mentality, she had to recognize that she is not perfect, had made some mistakes, and had been attached to a desired outcome. Many people get attached to outcomes in relationships versus looking at what is going on in the here and now. Her here and now was a broken heart with a man who continued to break his promises. Once she admitted her reality, sat with her mistake, and was willing to forgive herself, she was ready to reframe her narrative. I asked her to start with empowering phrases such as:

- "I can"
- "I may"
- "If I"
- "I could"
- "What if"

Her reframing was "What if I met a good guy?" Every single time she started to use a limited-belief phrase, she had to go back to "What if I met a good guy?" I wanted her to consider what it might look like to meet a nice guy. How would it feel? She needed to empower herself by teaching her mind to rephrase the negative into a positive. After a few weeks of this, she needed to learn that it was indeed possible. I asked her to start talking to both men and women in her office about the right people in their lives. She listened to people who had remarried and even one who had started over after an abusive relationship. We talked about the power in those examples, which showed her that it is okay to make mistakes. She used these examples to empower herself and affirm that things can and do get better.

The last part of her limiting-belief overhaul was agreeing to go on three different dates with nice guys. After the three dates, we went through her future-self exercise. She saw herself in a small white one-story home with flowers lining the walkway to her front door. She was happily married and, in her words, peaceful. She told her future self that the lesson she needed to learn was that she was capable of having the love of a good man. She also reminded herself to let go of her perceived failures as soon as she could, because they were the only thing standing between her and this beautiful life.

EXERCISE: SET GOALS

By now, you should be feeling empowered, educated, and ready to leave weak love in the rearview mirror. So, let's get on to the magic the future has in store for you, sister! We are going to outline precisely what you want in life and in love. Write down a real goal. It could be meeting a nice guy, losing the ten pounds you think is in your way, or getting married, if you are already on your way to loving strong.

Fill in the blanks.

What do you want?

_____

_____

Why do you want it?

_____

_____

When do you want to accomplish it?

_____

_____

How will you know you have accomplished it? What will it look like?

_____

_____

_____

Now that you know your goal, we can get down to business. Everything you do from this point on should be focused on your goal. If it is not helping you get to the goal, let it go. The next questions will help you reach your goal and maybe even help you find your true self along the way.

What do you like to do? Write down all of the things you enjoy.

1.
2.
3.
4.
5.

What are you good at?

1.
2.
3.
4.
5.

What is essential in your life to feel complete?

1.
2.

3.
4.
5.

What do you feel you were born to do?

1.
2.
3.
4.
5.

What makes you a great partner?

1.
2.
3.
4.
5.

What do you still need to work on to be the best version of yourself in a strong relationship?

1.
2.
3.
4.
5.

What are you grateful for in your life?

1.

2.
3.
4.
5.

What are your three most significant accomplishments in your life?

1.
2.
3.

What is the hardest thing you've had to overcome in your life?

_____

Who are your relationship role models?

_____

What major life transitions have you had that have played a part in your relationships?

_____

What three things in your life cause stress?

1.
2.
3.

What can you let go of to decrease your stress?

_____

List three things you are putting up with in your life at present.

1.
2.
3.

What is your major fear in life?

_____

What type of person motivates you?

_____

What type of person demotivates you?

_____

What are your core values?

_____

What core values will you look for in a future partner?

_____

What are your strengths in a relationship?

_____

What are your weaknesses in a relationship?

_____

What do you need to do right now to put yourself on a path to find strong, magical love?

_____

Everything you need to know is in these answers. Now all you have to do is decide to go for it and take action. You may have uncovered a few things you want to do some more work around. Don't be afraid to ask for help by bringing in a coach, therapist, or relationship council member to help keep you on track.

I hope that you have learned that you are uniquely you. You are made from not only your DNA but all of your life's experiences. Every hurt, monumental shift, and perceived setback has gotten you to where you are today. With each day that you learn more about yourself, you get closer and closer to finding your special person. Let go of the things that have not worked and forgive yourself for anything you are still holding on to. Love is the only thing that matters. As you can tell by now, I am a big fan of writing about feelings. You may be at a point today where you are ready to let go of some old loves. If you are, write a letter to the person or persons who are still taking up space in your mind. Tell them who you were when you met them, what you were looking for, and what you ultimately learned from your time with them. End with forgiving yourself and say aloud that you are letting them go. Keep freeing space until you feel like you are ready to move on. By understanding the lesson, you are continuing to regain your power.

EXERCISE: MAKE A VISION BOARD

I have asked you to shed a lot of old baggage. You have learned, loved, and forgiven yourself and others, and you deserve a reward. So, grab yourself a glass of cold pinot grigio and a few truffles, and find a comfy place where you can get creative. One of the things I like to do every year is make a vision board. It is one of the highlights of ringing in my new year. My husband used to laugh at me when I would bring out my markers, magazines, glue, and poster board. He thought I was wasting my time until he saw my goals beginning to come to fruition throughout the year. Now he does a vision board, too. Well, he humors me by cutting out pictures or looking through magazines as I choose my cutouts wisely. So, for our very last action item, I want to walk you through your own love-strong vision board.

Think about everything you have learned throughout this process. What kind of person do you want in your life? How do you want to feel? Where will the two of you live? Will you get married? What will the wedding look like? Where will you honeymoon or vacation? What activities will you do together? Who will the two of you hang out with? Will there be kids? If so, how many? What will they look like? Think about all of the possibilities while you plan out your vision for your love life.

Here are the supplies you will need to make your vision board:

- Beverage of choice
- Sweet or salty snack of choice…or both
- A giant poster or corkboard
- Glue, tape, or tacks
- Markers in colors you feel connected to (mine is always hot pink, and I tend to use a Sharpie)
- Five or ten magazines of your choice (about weddings, style, the home; *People*, *Veranda*, *Travel + Leisure*…or anything else you are pulled toward)

A vision board—or, as some people call it, a dream board—is a collage of images, goals, and affirmations designed by you to serve as a source of inspiration to attain your goals. Oprah Winfrey made the idea famous many years ago on her show. It was then that I got the bug. I love anything based on the law of attraction or anything else woo-woo.

When we are out of emotional, spiritual, and physical align-ment, our outside lives follow suit. Remember how I said you have to walk the walk and talk the talk? Well, with a vision board, you will be aligning your heart's desires with visual stimulation, but that is not all that it takes to make things happen. To make your dream board a reality, you can't just take a look at it every day and wish it into existence. Like everything else in the world, you have to have a plan of action. So, let's talk strategy here, ladies. You have started the process with this book, so what will happen from here?

Plan your work and work your plan. This means, decide what you need to do to make all of your visuals become a reality. Do you need to break up with someone you have been clinging to? Do you need to take a sabbatical to get your head straight and focus the next six months on yourself? Are you in therapy but concentrate only on the guy and not on yourself? Do you need to set boundaries?

Write down the top three things you need to do to achieve your overarching goal.

1.
2.
3.

Follow your mentors. Meaning, use other people who have gone through the same things you are trying to achieve to show you the way. Do your research and follow their leads. I offer countless online courses and webinars, and even do one-on-one coaching. There are people everywhere who have dedicated their lives to offering help from this specific step forward.

Take a risk, which means every week, do something out of your comfort zone. I don't mean bungee jumping off a cliff unless you are into that sort of thing. What I do mean is, try something—anything. When I wrote my first book many, many years ago I queried up to twenty agents a week and sometimes even in a day. I am an avid risk-taker today. I do it because it works. Here is an example. Just a few months ago, I was on a television panel with the fantastic DeVon Franklin talking about relationships. Off camera I spoke with him about this book you are reading now, along with an idea for a script I was writing.

During our conversation, I took a risk. I asked him if he would consider being my mentor. Yes, I asked him that. He was so gracious and offered me his contact information. We have been friends ever since. When you are attempting to take risks on this journey, find an accountability partner. Believe it or not, my last partner was a mother on my son's baseball team. After chatting one day, we both realized we are made from some of the same cloth. We are risk-takers. She was looking for a new job, and I was trying to pitch a TV show to a huge media company. I cannot tell you the fun we had every week sitting on the bleachers at the ball field and discussing the risks we had taken. Your risk may be to use a dating app or go out with a "nice guy." Perhaps it is to set a boundary with a family member or take a trip alone. Whatever it is, take the risk! A good life coach is always a home run as an accountability partner.

Leave your limiting beliefs at the door. They are not invited to your vision board party. It may be helpful to write them down before you get started. Then tear up the sheet and tell them to take a hike for this part of the process.

Okay, now that you're all pumped up, let's get started.

Vision Board Instructions

1. Get all of your supplies and find a comfy, creative space. It may be right smack in the middle of your living room or on your kitchen table. Next, look through the magazines and find pictures or words that depict the emotion you are looking to feel. Look for things that symbolize the life and partner you want to attract. Seek strong-love concepts such as commitment, marriage, respect, values, fun, or anything else that speaks to you. You may even want to use pictures of yourself on your board from a time when you felt happy and like you were living your best life. Keep the board simple and focused on the relationship goal you are after. If you have other goals for career or health, consider using a second board.

2. Now that you have cut out everything that speaks to you and you probably have paper scraps everywhere, let's look at your words of affirmation. Organize all of your words with the pictures that go with them. Are you happy with your piles? If not, don't worry; you can use your Sharpie to add anything that you feel is missing. Think of how you want to feel every day—and make sure you have those words handy.

3. Write your goals either on top of the page or in the middle. Then place the pictures and the words in a way that feels good to you. An example may be a goal of marriage. You may write, "I would like to find a loving husband and best friend." Outside of the words, you may put pictures of engagement rings, honeymoon spots, and perhaps even babies if they are in your future. When I did this, I added names that I liked for my future children. Once you have pasted or tacked everything to your board, you

will need to find somewhere to place it. You will want to visualize it every single day, so put in somewhere in your line of view. A good rule of practice would be to set aside some time during the day to meditate or do a guided visualization around your goals. Think about them positively and invitingly. Believe in them and remember the power you hold within you to make them happen. Invite them into your everyday life and talk about them with trusted friends and family. Get comfortable with expecting the magic that is coming to you and through you.

As time goes by, you will see the fruits of your labor with your dreams beginning to manifest. You will begin to feel such gratitude with each passing day. Write down in your journal the day and time any small or large dream comes to fruition. Doing so will lead you to see that Christmas comes all year long. My advice is to do a new board every year, as I do. It is powerful to see your ability to manifest your dreams and how the law of attraction is alive and thriving in you always.

CONCLUSION

*W*ell, I can hardly believe this, but we are nearing the end of our journey together. This book and my methodology have been a labor of divine love. I think back to all of the heartache and pizza I had to go through to make this all happen. Thank you for going on this extraordinary journey with me. I hope that you have already found strong love, and if you have not, that it is quickly on its way to you. Women today deserve the world. We are in a time in history when we can validate our worth and ask that society do the same. You have everything you need right now to get the love you want. You are perfectly and imperfectly you. Decide which parts you want to keep, and get rid of the beliefs, experiences, and guilt that no longer serve you.

You deserve to live your best life. You deserve to love strong and be intensely excited about your life. You have the power to do great things and to bring forth magical, strong love. Do not ever doubt yourself. Don't let anyone tell you that you are enough. Know when to walk away, and have the courage to know when to stay and do the work. Take your power back and never, ever give it away again.

I want to hear from you, so I have started the hashtags #tookmypowerback and #lovestrong to hear from my tribe about the monumental moments that have happened in their lives after they read this book. Let's all collectively decide to heal one another and empower one another along the way. Remember, I got you. And you, my girl, have this.

ACKNOWLEDGMENTS

As with every great story or idea that becomes a book, it takes a village of people to help you get to the finish line. I am always in awe of the people the universe puts in my path, and this book is no exception. For me, one of those people is DeVon Franklin. I had the fortunate pleasure of meeting him one day on set while we were both being featured on a panel to talk about relationships. I had just started laying out the methodology for this book and was in need of a nudge from the universe to tell me I was on the right path. His kind words of encouragement were just what I needed that day to kick-start this book into fruition. It is also through DeVon that I met my unbelievably talented book agent, Nena Madonia Oshman. Every author should be so fortunate as to have her in their corner. Nena, thank you for getting me and seeing the vision I had for this book. I also want to thank Wendy Sherman for her continued guidance and friendship. A special thank-you to Susie Orman Schnall for connecting me with the incomparable editing genius of Nicola Wheir. You are the yin to my yang. Thank you for always being there to listen to my ideas and to help my dreams become written words. Next stop, fiction! A special thank-you also to Rob and Ashley Eager for teaching me how to get my message out to the masses. I would also like to thank my family for their constant love and support. To my mother, Mary Dobbins, thank you for giving me the gift of writing and for always encouraging me to write about my feelings. Who knew you would one day through all of that analyzing create a relationship guru? To my brother, Jim Dobbins, for always supporting me. Thank you to all of my extended family trees in the Dobbins, Thomas, and Babul families. To my incredibly selfless husband, Jon Babul, thank you for loving me perfectly. To my children, Sophie Bleu and Weston Grey, I love you both to the moon and back. Now we can get that puppy. I am also eternally grateful for my tribe, my girlfriend gang, my mentors, and my relationship council: Trina, Denise, Jamie, Dana, Shelly, Courtney, Amy Nelie, Colleen, Traci, Sara, Chad, Blake, Uncle Bill, Uncle Albert, Tyler, Todd, Sam, Francie, Jess, Team G, Natalie, Leah, Christine, Cara, and last but not least, my FD tribe.